YOU
AND
YOUR
LANGUAGE

CHARLTON LAIRD

A SPECTRUM BOOK

PRENTICE-HALL, INC., ENGLEWOOD CLIFFS, N.J.

Library of Congress Cataloging in Publication Data

LAIRD, CHARLTON GRANT
  You and your language.

  (A Spectrum Book)
  1. English language. 2. English language—
Dialects. I. Title.
PE1075.L29   420   73–15654
ISBN 0–13–976977–3
ISBN 0–13–976969–2 (pbk.)

10 9 8 7 6 5 4 3 2 1

PRENTICE-HALL INTERNATIONAL, INC. (*London*)
PRENTICE-HALL OF AUSTRALIA PTY., LTD. (*Sydney*)
PRENTICE-HALL OF CANADA, LTD. (*Toronto*)
PRENTICE-HALL OF INDIA PRIVATE LIMITED (*New Delhi*)
PRENTICE-HALL OF JAPAN, INC. (*Tokyo*)

A word on language for

Helene

to whom I long ago gave my personal word

Contents

1

LANGUAGE

WHY YOU ACT LIKE
A HUMAN BEING

Go to a zoo and look about. You will be surrounded by creatures in many ways more able than any human being. The great cats can outrun you and outclaw you, the huge quadrupeds can outwork you, most of the birds can outsee you, the doglike creatures can outhear and outsmell you, the clumsiest sea mammal can outswim you. Even a spider that the janitor's mop has missed or an ant that has evaded the roach powder can perform miracles of delicacy and dexterity, and their speed, strength, and endurance per ounce put human athletes to shame. But you can leave or stay, as you like; they cannot. The otter is incarcerated and the spider is swept out, in part because their ancestors did not develop language, and you suffer neither indignity because your ancestors did. Looking about a zoo, one might be tempted to adapt John Bradford's words and say, "There, but for the grace of language, go I."

The answer may be that simple, or it may not be. There are other possibilities, and apologists for mankind have generally accepted them, assuming that human beings rule the world because they have more and better brains than have their fellow earth-inhabitants, that they should run the world because they practice a more noble morality than do other earthlings, because religion has been revealed to them,

1

or because they have divined higher truth. To most of us these appear as valid assumptions; for them we even have proofs of a sort, since other creatures fail tests made by men for men. Man can pass the tests he has made but he has never been asked to pass a test in friendliness devised by a porpoise, a test in landing on a twig designed by a wren, a test in artistic design devised by a spider, or a test in community living devised by an ant. In any event, braininess alone does not assure triumph or even survival. Ancient man had remarkable brains and had them for millennia before he amounted to much.

Language alone cannot account for everything, but it can work seeming miracles. There is a theory—plausible but obviously not provable—that although man could devise simple tools by fiddling with things, as other primates have, he could blunder out of the Old Stone Age only when he had language. Man, the somewhat specialized ape-creature, could scarcely have become what we call human without education, and education for civilized life relies on language. Without language, education is one child mimicking one adult at a time, a slow business. With language, complex teaching becomes possible, especially when supplemented with paralinguistic devices like writing, printing, and audio-visual aids.

To put all this in another way, language provided the platform for the current great evolution. The oldest growth we know was *physical evolution;* it took so long that astronomical time is inconceivable to human senses. Astronomers dabble in light-years, a concept ungraspably remote from most human apprehension. Physical evolution has left us with surroundings we are still probing for time and space; we believe our environment continues to evolve, but it may not have much changed pace, and if it has not, physical evolution in a human lifetime must be infinitesimal. *Biological evolution* was faster; measured in only millions of years, it has left us with a bewildering variety of beings from the monstrous to the microscopic, each with its own aptitudes.

Some millennia ago a third type of change developed, often called *social evolution.* Viewed in the long perspective of time, it has moved with startling rapidity and is accelerating. The evidence is so plenteous and statistics now balloon so rapidly they are scarcely worth quoting—infants can babble about space travel, long inconceivable; children can bandy problems that baffled philosophers; more great physicists are alive today than were known in the world prior to 1900; the United

States produces more real goods in one year than formerly the world could provide in a century. On and on.

Presumably, each of these great evolutionary trends was at once simple and complex. Something, or a complex of things, must have made each of them possible; physical evolution utilized energy, but the working of energy was so myriad that we can no longer speak of creation as less than a universe of universes. The life force may be reducible to one essential, to a chemical formula like DNA or to something electrical, but life as we know it is characterized by multiplicity. Similarly, social evolution may have sprung from some sort of *sine qua non,* and if so, language is probably the best guess. True, language alone could not have sufficed; at a minimum there had to be creatures that could develop and use language—presumably plankton could not have. But language may have been the sparking agent for social evolution, the means by which human evolution could move from ponderous biological change to volatile social change. At a minimum it was an ingredient.

A CHIMP AND THE PROBLEM OF LANGUAGE

A few years ago an infant chimpanzee, trusting but no doubt frightened, found herself being taken out of a crate by large, strange creatures. They did not hurt her. They even gave her food and drink, and let her snuggle down to sleep. The bumping and the sense of being interminably moved had stopped. But there was no mommy. Probably her skin itched from the dry air. She may have been hungry; there was food, but strange food. Probably she was cold, although she had a sort of nest. No doubt she was unhappy, desperately unhappy. If so, she would not have known the reason—that she had been born in a humid jungle, the child of jungle creatures, whereas now she was half a world away in a high American desert, watched over by a well-meaning pair of scientists who, at best, would have their shortcomings as chimpanzee parents.

That may be about all she knew. If she could recall the terrifying moments when she was captured, she would scarcely then, or at any time, have grasped how much her life was to be changed, nor what an important little bundle of primate she was to be. Because she could not conceive of speech, she could scarcely have imagined that she had started a course of training during which she was to become the first nonhuman being to learn what many scholars would call language.

She was not the first that somebody had tried to teach. Even before Darwin's theories of evolution, various people had noticed how humanoid the great apes are, and had tried to train them to speak. Some two centuries ago Lord Monboddo, a Scotch jurist, suggested that apes represented an earlier form of man, and imported an orangutan. The primate is said to have learned to play the flute, but he never learned to speak, and became an international joke. The satirist Thomas Love Peacock had a world of fun with him in *Melicourt: or Sir Oran Haut-ton.* Sir Oran, an Oriental gentleman—the *Haut-ton* of his cognomen was supposed to be French for "high-toned"—was famed for his taciturnity, since his only response was to bow, and for saving maidens by swinging from branch to branch. He was a tremendous success socially, and would probably have been elected to Parliament, except that some glimmering filtered into his dense skull. He sensed that the corrupt politicians who were promoting him were bad, and he made a shambles of the place.

Monboddo had followers. The primates are so much like human beings that all sorts of people tried to teach them all sorts of languages —French, Dutch, Russian, and others. None of these nonhuman primates learned more than a few syllables, mismouthed into incoherence. They may have been badly taught; poor old Monboddo was probably a better philosopher than animal-trainer, but some of the scientists who worked with nonhuman primates did such a good job that nobody could doubt the negative results: creatures like chimpanzees, orangutans, and gorillas cannot learn to speak. The assumption was that ape brains are not good enough.

There was another possible explanation, and several experimenters pursued it. Language requires brains and linguistic counters; what if the creatures had the right brains but were being given the wrong linguistic counters? Dissection did indeed reveal that most primates have an aural system so different from that of a human being that one might plausibly guess they could not speak even though they could think enough to do so. Accordingly, research workers tried to teach a nonhuman primate two-way communication using some other medium than sound—blocks, colors, and the like. One pair of investigators had the happy idea of using sign language, for after all, sign language is a language, not just a contrived system of shapes and colors.

They were Drs. Beatrice T. Gardner and R. Allen Gardner, comparative psychologists at the University of Nevada, whom we observed a few paragraphs back uncrating a frightened baby chimpanzee. They had acquired a federal grant for a research project, had bought the youngest chimpanzee they could, and in their back yard had fitted up a trailer home for a small occupant. They had learned ASL (American Sign Language) themselves, and had trained a laboratory crew to use it. The idea was that they would raise a young nonhuman primate, treating it as much as possible like a human child, except that it would never hear aural speech. Only sign language would be used, and as occasion warranted, the little chimp would be taught to sign. The Gardners named her Washoe, after the county where she had come to live, set her up in her home, and saw to it that she had companions all her waking hours who would cuddle her, feed her, converse with one another in sign language, and teach her to make signs.

She responded to the loving at once and soon to the signing. She could indicate that she wanted food or a sweet drink, that she wanted to be tickled, that she wanted to be tickled some more, and in a hurry. She was perhaps eleven months old when she started her life as a language trainee; within fifty-one months she had learned 132 attested signs—actually she knew more—and although she was never formally taught grammar, she was learning it. She could coordinate signs in what seem to be sentences, even complicated sentences. Being cold and knowing there were blankets in a locked cupboard, she asked the attendant to get the key so they could get a blanket out. She could ask and answer questions, understand directions, jabber with her playmates, and "talk" to herself in signs. She could use her langauge for objects she could only envisage; she would sign *dog* when she heard one bark. She is even said to have suggested to a visitor that the two of them go for a ride in an airplane she heard passing over.

She could develop meanings, and could become as angry at what she believed were language blunders as could any purist. Having been fed food from cans, she saw a picture of a can of beer and signed *food*. Her companion tried to correct her, signing that it was drink. Washoe would have none of this; she became sulky, searching through magazines to find more pictures of cans to prove she was right. On another occasion a companion used an impromptu flourish of the hand to indicate to another person that he wanted a cigarette. Washoe picked this up as a formal sign, and apparently knowing that matches were used to light either a cigarette or a stove, she developed a whole set of meanings for this sign associated with fires and lighting fires.

In short, Washoe was soon using sign language as any child uses the speech it inherits. She learned it rapidly; she even built it herself, and made it part of her unconscious life. She expected all human beings, and even other creatures, to understand her signs; when she went, at the end of the experiment, to live with a colony of chimpanzees, she expected them to understand ASL, and no doubt thought them very stupid when they did not. By the time she was five she had learned to communicate rather better, apparently, than do some human children of the same age, and this in spite of various handicaps—she started late, she had to use a linguistic system probably less adaptable than an oral-aural system, and she had no "native" speakers to imitate. She had no deaf-mute companions, and hence she must have learned a variety of "dialects," even a sort of sign-language baby-talk.*

Washoe raises questions, including this: If one nonhuman being can learn language, can others do the same? Washoe is now only one of several chimpanzees that have learned to sign, some apparently learning faster than she did. Some monkeys and foxes have devised many more signs than have wild chimpanzees, dozens of apparently meaningful calls and gestures. Whales can sing after a fashion, and sharks and porpoises can learn to do tricks and perform submarine tasks. If man can find an equivalent of sign language that dolphins can use, why should not they operate farms on the ocean floor? If robins, smart enough to outmaneuver hawks, can be taught a bird language, why should they not be asked to rid the earth of unwanted bugs? Washoe may not only be the first nonhuman to learn to use language; she may be the harbinger of a new age in which many creatures can communicate with man and with one another. That possibility is many years and thousands of experiments away, including this key experiment:

---

* The Gardners recorded the experiment in moving pictures and a daily log, best surveyed in their "Two-Way Communication with an Infant Chimpanzee," *Behavior of Nonhuman Primates*, ed. Allen M. Schrier and Fred Stollnitz (New York: Academic Press, 1971), pp. 117–84. They are careful not to claim that Washoe learned a language. I have endeavored to demonstrate that she was doing so; see "A Nonhuman Being Can Learn Language," *College Composition and Communication*, Vol. 23 (1972), pp. 142–54.

Can Washoe and other chimpanzee mothers teach signing naturally to their own babies without man's intervention? Can daughter chimps learn from their mothers, unconsciously, as human babies do? At this writing tests are underway, but the answer is not in.

WHAT IS LANGUAGE?

Whatever the implications of Washoe for worldwide ecosystems, her experience dramatizes questions in linguistics, including this one: What is language? For many purposes, a definition of language seems not very helpful. Few speakers can delineate language but they can identify it, at least with the simplest sort of definition, by pointing. To isolate language one has only to say, "It is what I am using now," and if that is not clear to the listener, the speaker has only to add, "Language is what you will use when you reply." Speakers think they know when they are using language and when they are not, and for practical purposes they are always right. For most purposes, that may be all they need to know.

But definitions are useful, and in questions like those raised by Washoe's learning, we need one. We know that language helped ape-like men to become human; we know that language promoted the growth of civilization, and we know that Washoe learned two-way communication. But can we define her communication as language, and hence as something that permits her and her kind to approach what we mean by human nature and civilized living? The thirty-seven distinct calls a Japanese monkey can make do suggest that he is smart as animals go; they do not suggest that he possesses one of the keys to being human. Washoe learned four times that many signs; does this mean only that she has four times as many units of communication as the Japanese monkey has, or does it mean that she now commands means that are available to all human beings, but until now have been available to none but human beings? The answer must appear through the definition of language.

Obviously, not all communication can be called language. A cow can make small mooing sounds that will keep a calf hiding in the brush; the moo is a sign, but it is not language. Some communication is not even deliberate. A snake that produces a buzzing with its tail may be making no conscious warning; it may be no more aware of purpose in a moving tail than is a dog with a similar wagging, but the resulting buzz becomes a sign. Languages do use such signs, both conscious and unconscious, but the signs used by animals in a wild state are few and inexact compared to those used in languages. One surmises that if the rattlesnake could multiply his signs by the hundreds, he still would not have a language.

Perhaps we can describe speech best by examining behavior that we recognize as language. It has often been defined about as follows: *Language is a complete, arbitrary system of expression and communication utilizing human sounds as symbols.* By this definition, Washoe was not using language, but obviously the definition, not Washoe, was at fault. She was not using sounds, but neither do other users of ASL; she was using signs, and sounds are not the only signs. Neither is Washoe human, but here again the definition is at fault; in the past, all known users of an extensive two-way system of communication have been human, but as soon as one nonhuman being learns to use such a system—as Washoe indisputably did—being classified as human is no longer one of the criteria. It is a characteristic, not a requisite; human beings have ten fingers, but nobody becomes inhuman because he loses a finger.

Thus some parts of a conventional definition fit most languages and users of language as we know them, but are not essential. Others seem to be so. One characteristic is that languages are systematic; they work through observable systems. Perhaps they need not; one can imagine that if the Japanese monkey could increase his 37 signs to 37,000 unsystematic signs he might have enough to express almost anything, but the fact is that no such linguistic system has been devised. Probably such a system, if it could be developed, could not be used; it would be too hard to learn and to remember. Apparently—and this must be part of the nature of all minds, including human minds—an assortment of devices extensive enough to serve as a language must have system in order to be usable.

Similarly, all known languages are in part arbitrary; that is, they are not entirely logical. They are not completely arbitrary; logic and all sorts of other things enter into them—mimicking of sounds, for example, as in the names *bobwhite* and *whippoorwill*—but apparently working languages must be essentially systematic, and to become systematic they must in part be arbitrary. Washoe could pass these requirements; she was taught an arbitrary system, and she learned to use her system in an arbitrary way. Similarly, Washoe used her signs as symbols; a dog will not recognize a picture of his master, but Washoe could; to her a picture of a dog or a distant bark was accepted as the dog itself.

If one criterion is crucial, it is probably the remaining one, embodied in the word *complete*, which in this specialized sense means that the medium is expandable toward infinity. That is, a competent user of a complete linguistic system can expand it so that it will serve him for any need. Spoken English is such a system; when the first sputnik was put into orbit no American had ever seen or otherwise experienced an orbiting object, but the language could be adapted at once to report the event, even to discuss it. At the end of her fifth year, Washoe did not command a system that was certainly complete; she could not discuss much. But neither can a five-year-old human child. The evidence seems to be that Washoe's signing system was growing rapidly, that it was as near to being complete as could be expected, that she probably could express almost anything she could conceive. Apparently, if her linguistic system was not yet complete, it promised to become so.

In short, no one can doubt that Washoe achieved extensive two-way communication. Language can, of course, be defined in such a way as to exclude Washoe's signing, but her system seems to be so much like what human beings use when they speak that it is better called language than anything else. Furthermore, it is enough like human speech so that we can plausibly assume that much of what language has done for man, Washoe's signing can do for chimpanzees and probably for other creatures. Thus we may need a new, three-part division of living creatures: those that can create a language and then use it, a category as yet made up only of human beings; those that have not created a language but can learn to use one, a category made up of chimpanzees, probably all primates, and some other species; and those that cannot use any more extensive means of communication than cries and gestures, along with a few conscious signs.

True, Washoe at five years could not use language as can a modern adult human primate; quite probably neither she nor any other of her race ever will. Human brains may well be the best brains ever developed in our universe, and the oral-aural system may be the best possible means of communication. One doubts that there will ever be a chimpanzee Shakespeare or a gibbon Aristotle, but Washoe has demonstrated that the uses of language can be spread beyond the human race, and she may have demonstrated something about the human race itself.

YOU, THE CHIMP, AND THE NATURE
OF LANGUAGE

Washoe's revelation is too recent and the evidence too fragmentary to be well assessed. We do not know, and are not likely soon to know, just what Washoe learned or how much she understood. She had a basic grasp of naming; she knew she had a name, that other people and things have names, and she recognized that the objects and the names can be used interchangeably. She could generalize—she knew that her feces were called *dirty* and she used the sign for other undesirable things—but whether she could generalize enough and then particularize enough to conceive of a dirty mind, we do not know. When she signed, "Washoe good," she probably meant that Washoe should be loved and deserved to be tickled or given some other reward, but how much was she investing the sign for *good* with moral judgments? She could express relationships; she recognized a certain garment as *Mrs. Gardner's coat*. Did she mean that the large affectionate creature who disseminated food had made the coat? That she had proprietary rights in the coat? That where the coat was Mrs. Gardner must have been? Or did she mean only that there was some kind of loose association between the two? She used predication; she would generate such sentences as "Let's you and I go outside and play hide-and-seek," and she seemed to have some preference for the order subject, verb, and complement in such sequences, but often one can only surmise what her structures may have been.

Even so, Washoe's acquisition of language raises questions about your speech and mine. Philosophers have long seen that there must be something universal in language, although observed superficially, languages are different, so different that a second or a third language, if it is to be acquired, must be learned. But at some level languages must have likenesses. Speech must be the embodiment of something that involves being human; it must grow in part from the way brains work, from the ways human beings use language to live with. And particularly in recent years linguists like Noam Chomsky have been pointing out that language is so rich and diverse that no mind could assemble and order it if there were not something innate in mankind that provides patterns for sorting and classifying linguistic data.

Interestingly, some of the best candidates for these language universals—to which we shall return—are characteristics of Washoe's learning. We have seen that she loved names, wanted names for things, and could readily build proper names into common nouns. She could deal with symbols. She understood modification, as in *Mrs. Gardner's coat*. She could conceive the parts of conventional predication, that something exists, that it has identifiable qualities, that it can act or be acted upon. That is, as there must be a level where all human brains work along common lines, there must also be a level where human brains and chimpanzee brains work in common. Whether the two levels are the same we do not know, and may never know.

2

LANGUAGE
AS EDUCATED BREATH

"S-s-s-s-s-s!" (Or perhaps one should write, "Th-th-th-th-th!" Anyhow, a gander can do it.)

"G-r-r-r-r-r-r!" (However you try to spell it, dogs can growl and snarl.)

Stemming from an elemental need, these noises serve a primitive want, warning as self-defense. They mean, "Keep your distance or I attack." If the warning fails, the creature can then only fight or flee. A dog can make a few other sounds, which we suggest by words like *bark, bay, whine,* and *whimper.* Such utterances communicate somewhat more—that attack is being considered but is not yet decided upon, that the animal is excited, or in pain, or is trapped, or humiliated and wants help or sympathy. But he cannot say much with his yappings; he will go through all sorts of antics to communicate—leaping, flouncing, rolling over, offering his paw, slinking with his tail between his legs. Even the gander, goose that he is, communicates by means other than hissing—thrusting out his neck, opening his bill, and threatening with his wings. Many creatures use both noise and gesture in their efforts to say something, but understandably they find gesture the more expressive of the two.

Some creatures have developed bodily movement into elaborate systems. Bees, for instance, have more intelligence per milligram than most other beings—except possibly angels, who presumably weigh nothing—probably more per avoirdupois than men. They have societies, train their young for specific tasks, know how to provide for the future, build elaborate storage vaults, use mutual defense, have devices for population control, and have developed a complicated signal system. A bee worker, waiting to go out for a load of pollen or honey, will stroke the bodies of returning workers, presumably learning in what direction the incoming load was found, how far away it is, perhaps something about it. What thinking takes place we do not know: Does the incoming worker consciously manipulate his body to reveal facts through formalized symbols? How much does the "debriefing" bee have to think to interpret the bodily evidence that he senses in his stroking? Can he ask questions and can the incoming bee reply? Do the workers make sounds inaudible to us? We do not know; the queen bee can make a piping sound, but she does not vary it much and uses it only for limited purposes.

Clearly, most creatures have limited means of expression. Communication is not an elemental need, as are food and sex. Walt Kelley's loquacious worms to the contrary, the simpler creatures seem not to feel the need to communicate and have no organs specialized for such purposes. They have means of ingesting and digesting food, specialized organs to excrete waste, to induce conception, to give birth. If you were devising a creature, you would provide it with specialized devices for expression and comprehension; man has done so while inventing "electric brains," but the Lord in his wisdom apparently preferred not to do this. He preferred to let life work out what it needs, and because for millions of years creatures had little communal life, no organs developed for the purpose. Those we have were utilized late; when the need to communicate grew, too late for specialized means to develop, complex organisms could only convert to communication members they already had—organs that had grown for some more elemental use. Sensitivity to sound antedated speech sounds by eons. Bees must have used bodies and feet before they learned to spot food sources with them. We breathed with lungs before we could talk using a column of air.

Biologically, then, communication was late, and when it became a felt need, there were no adequate means to fill the need. But communication, not an elemental necessity, has in a sense become for social creatures the greatest need; modern man finds mutual comprehension more difficult than getting something to eat. To satisfy this late but growing appetite, some creatures acquired the senses: taste, smell, touch, hearing, and sight. We are probably safe in assuming that all complex creatures have tried to use all of them that they possess, but in most creatures most of these means have not adapted readily to two-way communication. Taste and smell provide mainly one-way signals, although bitterness may save a plant from being eaten and some creatures can emit a smell that is about the defensive equivalent of the gander's hiss. Touch is eloquent, but not highly varied, and useless except with contact. Sight and gesture served most creatures best, but one discovery, perhaps more than any other, permitted the descendants of certain arboreal apes to become human—a column of air can be so governed as to produce a seemingly infinite variety of controllable sound. And hearing has advantages, even over sight; it can work in the dark, the dark of night or the dark of a cave. It can move around obstacles, and it functions automatically in all directions and can continue even though its user is working, fighting, or making love.

Thus man is not the only creature to devise a signal system. Nor, as we have seen in the previous chapter, does he possess the only brain good enough to deal with language. But he is apparently unique in having devised means to control and vary a column of air so that language in its infinite multiplicity became possible. Logically, gesture and sight might have seemed more promising; bodily movement is older and must have seemed more adaptable. But a column of air can be varied by a concatenation of devices that nobody would have been likely to associate mentally; their use in combination had to be worked out.

HOW YOU EDUCATE YOUR BREATH: VOWELS

Natural breath is unobstructed air flowing into the lungs and out. Viewed as a physical act, human speech is this same column of air, mainly the outgoing column, as it is variously disturbed through the re-education of certain body parts.

To see how uneducated air becomes meaningful sound, let us follow air leaving the lungs. The diaphragm, a tough membrane separating the lung cavity from the stomach cavity, is being raised; at the same time the intercostal muscles contract slowly, reducing the rib cage. These actions work like a bellows to force air from the lungs into a tube known as the trachea and thence into the throat through a gate-like assemblage called the *larynx,* or more commonly the *voice box* or *Adam's apple*—the legend was that a gobbet of the forbidden fruit stuck in Adam's throat. This larynx is a complex of cartilage, muscles, and membranes, including the vocal cords and vocal folds. Closed, these membranes exclude liquids and solids from the lungs, directing them to the stomach. Open, they allow breathing.

But the vocal folds and cords need not be either completely open or closed. If they are closed only enough to provide friction, air forced strongly through the larynx, will produce the whisper sound associated with the letter *h,* written /h/. If the cords are closed somewhat more they vibrate and set the whole column of air to vibrating. That is what a vowel is—most vowels, anyhow—the sound of a vibrating flow of air, the flow not much restricted except in the voice box. The phenomenon is called *voicing;* one can hear it by saying a vowel while stopping his ears. The pitch of this sound can be raised or lowered by contracting or relaxing the pull on the vocal cords. That is, the voice box—which might more accurately be called the *voicing box*—is like a reed instrument in that it sets up vibration because of the air passing through it, but more like a violin or ukelele in that the pitch of the vibration can be changed by tension on the strings.

The easiest way to make a vowel is to open the mouth and let the voiced column of air come. This is what happens when a baby squalls, and when an adult makes the sound with the mouth open and relaxed the result is the vowel commonly called broad Italian *a,* written /ɑ/. In making this sound, the lower jaw will drop somewhat, the lips will be well open and only slightly rounded, the pitch of the voice will be relatively low, and the sound will seem to center low in the mouth and about halfway back. Such changes will accompany any vowel you make, because agents like the jaw, lips, and tongue can move so as to alter the contour of the mouth, throat, and nose as a resonance chamber. To see how this goes, say slowly and repeatedly, *haul eels.* You will notice that for the first word the tongue pulls back, and the sound seems to come from as far back in the mouth as you can speak. The mouth opening is large and the pitch of the vowel low. We shall write this sound with a *c* upside down /ɔ/. For *eels* the tongue moves forward and up, narrowing the resonance passage and—although you can only

infer this, because you will not be conscious of change in the voice box
—the vocal cords will shorten so that the pitch of the vowel is high.
You will have made the highest front vowel, which we write /ij/.
These, then, are the limits of vowels, from *low back* /ɔ/ to *high front*
/ij/. Each vowel sound is different from the others in many ways, but
the most notable distinction involves the position of the tongue, which
has much to do with the sound being low or high, back or front. The
pitch of the vowels will seem to go with tongue position automatically,
because low pitch will accompany low back positions, and pitch will
rise as the vowel moves forward or upward. Accordingly, vowels are
best distinguished, although not completely described, by position.

That is, vowels can be thought of as back, mid, or front—*mid* being
a technical term placing a sound roughly midway between two others
—and low, mid, or high. They can be made from just in front of the
throat to just back of the teeth, and they may seem to center either on
the floor of the mouth, along its roof, or somewhere toward the middle.
The following diagram, greatly simplified, may help. The symbols not
already identified will be described below.

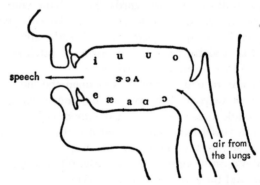

A sequence of vowels seems to follow along the floor of the mouth.
We have identified /ɔ/ as the sound farthest back and lowest in tone,
heard in *awk, taught.* In front of it is the relaxed vowel /ɑ/, as in *hot,
top.* (We are, of course, considering *sound,* not spelling; only a few
words having the sound /ɑ/ are spelled with *a,* mostly if a Latin sound
is preserved, as in one pronunciation of *amen*). In front of /ɑ/ and a
bit higher is /a/ as in one pronunciation of *father, ask.* This sound
is so near to /ɑ/ and so mingled with it in most American dialects that
in rough transcription one symbol can serve for both. The sound /a/

approximates that in *park* and *car* when such words are pronounced with an *r*-sound, although the sounds in *park the car* are somewhat higher and farther front than /a/. A little in front of /a/ is /æ/, as in *and* and *hat*, a very common sound in English, especially in American English outside New England, and it is growing there and in even British English, where it was long frowned upon as a supposed Americanism. Considerably above /æ/ and somewhat forward is /e/, as in *get* and *dead*. Still higher, almost by the upper front teeth, is /i/ as in *tin, hill*.

A similar sequence follows along the roof of the mouth, similar in that this sequence too can be described as going forward and upward. We can start with the same low back vowel, /ɔ/ as in *awk*. Considerably above it and somewhat forward is /o/, as in *open* and *ode*. In front of it is /ʊ/ as in *good*, and in front of that /u/ as in *rude, too*. These two sounds alternate by dialect in a few words; *roof* can be pronounced /rʊf/ or /ruf/, *soot* can be /sʊt/ or /sut/. Farthest front is /i/. That is, two sequences of vowels can be thought of as following a low curve or a high curve from /ɔ/, low back, to /i/, high front.

Vowel sounds can center elsewhere in the mouth. In English not many do, but a few occur toward the middle, of which the most common is written /ə/, with *e* upside down. This is a very slack vowel, with little stress. English is a heavily stressed language, but because vowels accented in a word or stressed as prominent syllables in a phrase are hit hard, other vowels tend to weaken, even to disappear. For example, *the* in the sequence "It is quite *the* thing to do," will be pronounced rather as though it were spelled *thee*. On the other hand, in the nonchalance of conversation the vowel is usually reduced to little more than a gentle grunt, and before a word beginning with a vowel to nothing at all, as in *th' answer*. This sort of thing has been going on for a long time. The word *about* was formerly *on-butan*, meaning "on the outside," with all three vowels carrying some stress and each with its own character. Now the third vowel is gone, and the /n/ with it. The initial vowel, which has lost its stress, has become the relaxed /ə/, and many speakers drop it entirely and say *'bout a dozen*.

Thus the sound /ə/, called *schwa*, has become the most used sound in English, especially in American English. It may be used as the vowel in both prefixes (*about, among, untrue*) and suffixes, along with inflectional endings (*solvent, burden, rooted*) in many dialects, although not in all. In English, almost any vowel that loses its accent, whether from a change in the pronunciation of a word or the varying stress of speech, can become schwa, and at least in American English many of them do. Schwa is also the most rapidly growing sound. In English as in many languages, syllables are always dropping out, and before they disappear completely schwa is likely to be used for a time. Furthermore, the English language has been a great borrower of words, and when words are borrowed they very frequently undergo change of stress—with more vowels losing their quality and becoming schwa. Thus schwa is a rag-bag of vowels losing their stress, many on the way to extinction.

Some other sounds can be heard toward the middle of the mouth. Among these is a relaxed sound in front of schwa, written /ɨ/; standard speakers pronounce *get* /get/, but many will say /git/ or use the relaxed sound, somewhat farther back, written as an *i* with a bar through it /ɨ/. The sound before a final *r* is enough like schwa so that it can be written /ə/, as in *seller* /selər/ and *hillier* /hiliər/ in dialects where a terminal *r* is pronounced. There is a stressed sound, also, in the middle of the mouth; it is often written as schwa, but it is a bit higher and farther back than /ə/, and many scholars observe this distinction and write it with an inverted *v* /ʌ/ as in *cup* /kʌp/. For dialects having a sound farther forward, notably in England, Canada, and New England, the sound in a word like *seller* can be written /ɝ/.

The discussion above assumes that a vowel is one sound, that it begins in a certain way, continues that way, and ends without change. This is of course not true; the pose was adopted for simplicity. Most vowels can be made in several ways. For example, /ə/ can be made higher or lower than /ʌ/, farther back or farther forward. I have tried to describe the vowels as many Americans make them, but there will be individual variations. Of course these variations have limits; nobody can make /i/ like /ɔ/ or /ɔ/ like /i/. Furthermore, making a pure vowel is almost impossible and not necessarily desirable—although vowels having little internal change are commonly called pure—but Modern English is notable for its shifting sounds within vowels. Almost every vowel will have some incoming or outgoing glide, or both, although many of these glides are so slight or so much the peculiarity of an individual speaker that they can be ignored here. Some cannot be.

We have noticed that English has heavy and light stresses. A heavy stress is likely to be accompanied by increased length, some rise in pitch and volume, and a notable glide. Thus the vowel in *heat* starts much like the vowel in *hit*, but it is longer, higher, and has more off-glide. It can be written conveniently by recognizing this glide as in *heat* /hijt/. Similarly, we could distinguish *get* /get/ from *gate* by adding a glide for *gate* /gejt/. One glide after /o/ can produce the sound in *boil* /boil/, but another glide is farther back, so that *boat* can be written /bout/. In-glides are unusually varied; a word like *house* can be transcribed /haus/, /haʊs/, /hæʊs/, or /heʊs/, depending on the dialect. Similarly, *ride* can be suggested by /rɑid/ or /raid/. For *news* some speakers say /nuz/, some /niuz/.

EDUCATING YOUR BREATH: CONSONANTS

We have seen that a vowel results from a vibrating column of air, altered by the lips and a resonance chamber, although not much disturbed otherwise. But a column of air can be disturbed; it can be redirected, restricted, even stopped. Let us try other ways of disrupting the flow of air.

Start with a voiced column of air such as you would use for a vowel. Assume you are saying *odd;* you would probably be using the broad Italian *a* we have written /ɑ/, although some speakers would use /ɔ/. Now stop the flow of air by raising your tongue to the roof of your mouth back of the teeth while still voicing, let the air build up a little pressure, and then let it go. You will form the terminal sound in *odd* or *god*, which we may write /d/. It was made by a stop followed by a small explosion; we can call it a voiced *stop* or *plosive*. The tongue stopped the air in front of the teeth or at the alveolar ridge; we can call it a predental or alveolar stop. Such a sound is not one thing; in my own idiolect—that is, my own way of speaking, for everybody has his own—if I am to say *Damn it* I start by putting the tongue well back of the teeth and pushing the tongue up so that it flattens a bit. If I pronounce the *d* in *riding,* only the tip of the tongue comes up to give the alveolar ridge a quick flick. If I say *head,* the *d*-sound is made somewhat forward, but with the tongue flattened rather more than in *riding,* not so much as in *Damn.* In fact, if I watch myself in the mirror, and try other combinations such as *cheddar* and *sinned,* so that the /d/ is associated with various sounds, I find I pronounce /d/ in at least a dozen different ways, with differences that could be detected in photographs of sound waves, although most people could not hear the differences—and I am not sure I can make them consistently.

This may be a good point at which to introduce an idea that has been skirted, that of the *phoneme*. When scholars started trying to record sound, they used various symbols. Understandably, the result was bedlam. Accordingly, the International Phonetic Alphabet (abbreviated to IPA) was devised and widely used. The idea was that for any language sound a human being could make there would be one symbol the world over. This device helped, but language is so varied that IPA now comprises more than five hundred symbols, and new symbols constantly become necessary as new languages are recorded and old ones are restudied.

But sounds exist not only in the speech organs. They exist also in the mind, and it is possible to recognize with a symbol what people assume a sound to be. This is what I was doing above, when I wrote a sound as /d/, although I was aware that I make several sounds as voiced predentals. That is, a symbol written between slant lines is a *phoneme;* it represents a spread of sound, the spread that users of a language are likely to accept as one thing. Thus a phoneme will not be the same for all languages, or even for the same language at all times. It will be what the speakers of a language at a given time recognize as a single sound. Meanwhile, when we must record sound more accurately, we can use IPA; English sounds associated with spellings *r* can be written [r], [R], [ɹ], or in several other ways (IPA symbols are enclosed within brackets) but for our purposes phonemes are likely to be precise enough most of the time, and using them simplifies the whole process of talking about language. Naturally, vowels are likely to include even more varied spreads of sound within a phoneme than do consonants like /d/.

Now let us try more consonants. Starting with a column of air not voiced, and stopping the flow of air at the teeth or just back of them, as in *tint*, you will get /t/, the voiceless stop corresponding to the voiced /d/, although actually, in most idiolects the tongue is a little farther forward for /t/ than for /d/. Now, if you stop a voiced column of air with both lips you will get /b/ as in *bib*, and with an unvoiced column, /p/ as in *pip*. If you stop the air farther back, with the tongue raised so that it spreads against the roof of the mouth on what is called the palate, you will make the palatal stops, /g/ voiced as in *good*, /k/ voiceless as in *can*.

But sounds can be restricted without being stopped completely. If you start with a vibrating column of air and restrict it by placing your upper teeth against your lower lip you will make /v/ as in *leave*, called a *voiced fricative*. The corresponding voiceless fricative is /f/, as in *leaf*. Restricting the air at the alveolar ridge, back of the teeth, produces /ð/ voiced as in *this*, voiceless /θ/ as in *think*. If you stop the air still farther back, against the palate, you will produce two fricative sounds found in Old English but now mostly lost, voiceless /χ/, much like the German hackle, rather like a continuing *k-k-k-k*, and voiced /ɣ/, rather like a continuing *g-g-g-g*. If the opening into the mouth is closed and the column of air voiced and directed through the nose, nasal consonants can be formed with the tongue in essentially the same three positions, /m/ as in *mama* with the lips closed, /n/ as in *nan* with the tongue at the alveolar ridge, and /ŋ/ farther back as in *sing*. Obviously, these consonants make a pattern:

	stops		*fricatives*		*nasals*
	(V)	(U)	(V)	(U)	
At the lips	/b/	/p/	/v/	/f/	/m/
At the teeth or alveolar ridge	/d/	/t/	/ð/	/θ/	/n/
At the palate	/g/	/k/	(lost)		/ŋ/

Consonant quadrangles like this one are common in languages because voicing or unvoicing are universal in human speech and because consonants have to be made with some sort of obstructing mechanism, of which not many are available. The lips and teeth are obvious points of stoppage. The tongue does most of the remaining job, and the readiest uses of it are to thrust forward or push up, not so far forward. If it is retracted, the air hisses through the nearly closed teeth, producing /ž/ voiced as in *measure*, /š/ voiceless as in *fish*. If it is raised in two ridges with a trough between and the air is directed like a jet toward the upper front teeth, the result is /z/ voiced as in *please, his*, and /s/ voiceless as in *siss*. The tip of the tongue can be made to vibrate, producing a trilled *r*, a sound now little used in English, or it can be raised against the roof of the mouth to produce the apical *r* of Spanish, or it can be bunched toward the center of the mouth as it is for the common English *r*, written /r/. It can be made to fill so much of the mouth that the air flows around it both ways in what is called a *lateral*, /l/ as in *lily*. Some of these sounds like /l/ and /r/ are rather more like vowels than consonants, the flow of air is restricted so little. The term *semivowel* is variously used for these and other sounds, including those associated with *w* as in *water* and *sewer*, written /w/, a voiceless semi-vowel, made with rounded lips.

Such sounds as these can be combined. The consonants /s/ and /k/ are written in sequence, as in *scale* /skejl/, but consonants may become so blended that they are given a single symbol. One such combination, called an *affricate*, begins with a plosive and continues as a fricative. For example, the first and last sound in *judge* seems to start with a /d/ and go on to a /ž/; it is commonly written /ǰ/. If the sound is voiceless as in *church*, it is written /č/. Some sounds will seem to move from place to place, and hence are called *glides;* they include /j/, the initial sound of *young*. As a matter of fact, many sounds—except those firmly fixed, /p/ and /b/ made at the teeth, for example—develop more or less noticeable glides during the flow of speech.

NOW TO SAY A WORD

Let us see how this sort of thing works, and that the description will not drag on for pages, let us choose one short word, *boasting*. It will be preceded by a slight reduction of the lung cavity, countless small mus-cles that control the diaphragm and the ribs contracting so as to give a continuing flow of air. Several other changes must accompany this flow of breath; the uvula flaps shut to keep the air from flowing into the nose; the vocal cords contract a bit, along with other adaptive changes in the larynx, and if the lips are not closed they must be. A little, but only a little pressure is built up; the air is flowing and has no place to go. Suddenly the lips part, the jaw lowers, the tongue flattens slightly, enough to give free passage to the column of air set vibrating by the vocal cords. The sound is /b/.

It must last only a fraction of a second. The mouth complex has been relaxed, but now muscles become tenser all through the throat and face. The column of vibrating air continues, but is restricted in a shifting way. The tongue pulls backward and upward, narrowing the channel through which the air flows, while the jaw drops somewhat more and the back of the throat pulls down still farther. The lips rise and round. Meanwhile the uvula remains closed and the vocal cords continue to vibrate. But this combination is only nicely started when it shifts. The lips round even more, but the tongue, which had drawn back as though the tip were being compressed, now shifts forward as though it were being squeezed at the root; the throat rises, as does the jaw. That is, a high mid vowel is being formed, followed by a glide, the sound we have written /ou/.

After a fraction of a second, a complex of movements begins. The flow of air continues, but the voicing stops. The jaw rises until the teeth almost close. The lips lose all their rounding and spread wide, reducing the opening to a slit. The tongue darts forward; the tip is pressed firmly against the roots of the lower teeth; the tongue arches up and the back part of it spreads so as to prevent air from going past on either side. The body of the tongue bunches toward the sides and draws down sharply along the center line to make a V-like trough. The air whistles through this trough, striking the upper teeth to make the fricative /s/. Quite suddenly the tongue changes all this; the bulk of the tongue drops and spreads even more to the sides while the tip flips up to flick the roof of the mouth just back of the teeth. The air is dammed completely, and then let go to form the sound /t/.

Once more there are abrupt changes. The flow of air keeps coming while the muscles of the thorax continue their carefully restrained contraction, but now the larynx has made its minute adjustments to start the voicing again. The lips part a bit more, the lower jaw drops, the muscles of the throat grow tenser, and the tongue executes another of its acrobatic contortions. The tip had been thrust out, long and thin; now it drops and flattens, but remains far front filling the space back of the lower teeth. The result is a high, front vowel /i/.

Imperceptibly, the vowel ends. The tongue pulls in upon itself, becoming bunched toward the back and rather high, so that access into the mouth cavity is stopped completely. The uvula flips open. The vibrating air that had previously been going out through the mouth is now diverted through the nose, where its pitch and intensity are heightened by the narrow nasal passages and by some tightening of the vocal cords. The lips are spread wide and the throat muscles tensen. The sound is /ŋ/, and it continues until all at once the diaphragm and the thorax muscles stop propelling air, the larynx relaxes, the uvula flips shut, and the muscles of the lips and throat become slack. The word is finished. (If the speaker is one of those who end a word like *boasting* with an /n/, the tongue would have flattened toward the front and spread so that it would stop the flow of air at the alveolar ridge. The same speaker might use /ə/ rather than /i/, occasioning a different sequence of muscle movements.)

That, in a simplified way, is what happens when we use the so-called organs of speech instead of gesture as a means of communicating. Small wonder that, if Washoe's fellow chimps did not have the right sort of tongue and vocal chords, they could never learn to do it. Nor need we wonder that a child takes months, even years, to teach the tongue all the tricks it must learn, especially because he does not think of himself as a teacher, or know what a pedagogue he must become. If he did, he might well settle for gestures, which as Washoe demonstrated, can be made to serve, at least within limits.

3

LANGUAGE
AS ANSWER TO A NEED

NAMING

"There's the doughnut!"
"Where? I don't see—."
"To the left. Beyond Mae West."

Seconds later, both the doughnut and the bulbous structure were out of sight. Conversations like this were common when astronauts were orbiting the moon, photographing the terrain, and spotting their proposed landing site. The moon explorers had responded as apparently have all explorers everywhere to the need for naming. These particular landmarks had not been learned as part of astronautical training; the "doughnut" and "Mae West" do not appear on any drawn map. The astronauts themselves had named the shapes spontaneously, and these natural names soon proved to be the best ones. They did not need to be learned because they reflected the way the astronauts had seen the formations. Details of the terrain could thus be readily spotted, even though the spotter was traveling at thousands of miles an hour.

Persons and objects everywhere acquire names. Working men call one another *Red, Shorty,* and *Tex,* and refer to the employer as *The Boss* or *The Old Man.* A workman needing a pipe wrench is not likely to say, "You with the shock of reddish hair over your left eye, I need the appropriate implement to break this joint." He prefers to say, "Hey Red. Toss me the Stillson." And the need was probably not less—nor did the method apparently differ much—when the subject of a cry was a pterodactyl to be chased from the family hearth or a platypus to be speared.

Seldom can we witness natural naming. Parents plan names for expected offspring, and children name their pups and kittens, even their dolls and playthings, but naming of this sort can reflect custom as well as need. Parents name their children gleefully; they may even do it soberly and thoughtfully, but they know that this is one of the things you do, maybe even one of the rewards of having a baby. But most of them do not consciously weigh the advantages of naming against the trials, even the danger, that would dog a nameless infant. As happens so frequently, need has crystallized in convention; not often can we witness naming as a natural and spontaneous response, as with the orbiters of the moon. But an examination of modern names will suggest that naming goes back to the earliest creatures we can call human—and perhaps even farther back, for we might recall that Washoe understood names, and readily bestowed them. Modern names provide internal evidence as to the manners in which they were given, and forms of names suggest the same sort of name-giving—the technical term is *onomastics*—that we observed among moon-orbiters.

NAMES FOR YOU AND ME

Consider the names of people. Many families are known as *White, Black, Green, Brown, Gray,* and even *Blunt, Blount,* and *Blondell* (involving *blond*), from the color of hair, eyes, and skin. Such surnames doubtless arose from such designations as *Eric the Red* and *Harold Fairhair.* There are *Little,* and *Long* for tall (with its variant *Lang*), as well as *Short,* which through French could be *Curt,* although that term was confused with *Curtis,* probably a form of *courteous.* A lame man could be *Cruikshank* and a smart man *Sharp. Grossteste* (he was a bishop) is only the French form of *Broadhead.* A man could be free (*Fry, Frye*). People were named from their occupations; there are multitudinous *Smiths, Millers, Fishers, Hunters, Taylors, Butlers, Farmers, Butchers, Shepherds* (however spelled), *Haywards* (another sort of rural patrolman), *Merchants, Bowers, Cooks, Bakers, Baxters, Brewers,*

Porters, Masons, Carpenters, Cowards, Glovers, Coopers, Foresters, Wrights, Drapers, Webbs, Colliers, Sergeants, Weavers, Fletchers (arrow-makers), on and on. When similar names reflect other languages one has *Schmidt* (Smith), *Bailey* or *Bailies* (bailiff), *Bauer* (farm laborer), *Ritter* (horseman), *Fischer* (fisherman), *Marchand* (merchant), *Moliere* or *Molina* or *Molinari* or *Milner* or *Mullner* or any of dozens of variants upon the word that is *miller* in English. Of course one could acquire the surname *Pope, Bishop, King, Cesar, Baron, Saint, Priest,* or *Lord* without being one or having such an ancestor; any connection, however tenuous, with an exalted personage might serve to exalt an adherent or even a menial, as in *Nevin* (Neven, Nivens), which means "little saint" in Welsh. People could be named, also, for their origin—*English, Dutch, French, Welsh* (Wallis, Wallace), *Scott, Irish, Cornish.*

People could be named for their homes. *Attwood* is presumably the compression of *at the wood,* and other forms are *Wood, Woods, Forest, Grove, Firth, Shaw, Holt, Hurst* and *Hearst, Weald, Lund* (Old Norse), *Coed* (Welsh) as in *Cottswold.* In German *Attwood* becomes *Zumwalt* (*zu dem Walt*); the same idea becomes *du Bois* in French and *Del Monte* in Spanish—although that could mean *from the mountain—* and various names incorporating *Madera* and *Selva.*

Woods were not the only phenomena that identified homes. Especially common were flat pieces of ground; *Field* appears in dozens of compounds—*Duffield* (either from-the-field or dove field), *Fielding* (field dweller), *Hatfield* (heather-field), *Summerfield* (a field usable only in the summer). Perhaps the most common were forms of *lea* however spelled (*Lee, Lea, Ley, Leigh, Legh, Leighs*) from Old English *leah,* meaning an open or somewhat wooded place. In unaccented syllables it has been reduced to something like *-ley* or *-ly,* as in *Akeley* or *Oakley* (oak clearing), *Ashly, Ashley* (ash clearing), *Aspley* (aspen clearing), *Astley* (eastern wood clearing), *Attlee* and *Atley, Audley,* and on through the alphabet. There are *Meadows* and *Hickinbothams* (low ground with oak trees), *Hulses* (hollows), *Fenns,* with combinations like *Fennwick* (swamp dairy farm), *Fenton,* and *Fenby.*

Elevations are common. *Hill* combines into *Hilton, Haverhill, Hillam*—although probably not *Hilliard* or *Hillier,* because a *hillier* was a roofer. *Higby* can be a high place, and so can *Higham. Howe* can be another form of *high,* for any sort of high grounds, spelled also *Ho* and *Haw,* but these get mixed up with *Hawes* and *Haughs* from a neck of land, and *Hughes, Hewes,* which in various spellings may refer to nobility of mind. *Mount* and *Mound* are not uncommon, and are combined in names like *Mountbaden,* even as the first element of *Mowbray.* The modern term *dune* appears in *Dunstan* (hill-stone) and *Dunster* (in which both elements mean hill), but combinations with -*don,* -*doun,* and even -*ton* can be one of many things, as we shall see below. There are names like *Peak* and *Pike* (forms of the same word), *cliff* as in *Cleveland* and *Suttcliffe,* Old English *hrych* in *Ridge* and *Reigate,* and many more. A little girl is said to have been called *Precipice* after her Uncle Cliff, whose name may have come from *Clifford,* which combines a curious linking, since fords are not usually cliffs. Likewise, rivers and the need to do something about them can be fruitful of names, with terms like *Ford* and *Bridge,* which are especially common in compounds, *Depford, Oxford, Cambridge,* thousands of them. *River* itself is not very frequent because the word is late in English, but people called *Flood, Brook* or *Brooks, Beck, Waters, Pond,* and *Lake* are common enough. Most of these terms stem from the native Old English tradition, but even more interesting are the Celtic survivals, especially for rivers.

THOSE ONOMASTIC CELTS

The Celts migrated from Eastern Europe, and like other conquering and exploring folk they scattered place-names wherever they went. They apparently moved in waves, the different waves having different dialects. Thus new Celtic names were strewn on older Celtic names, and after the Celts came various Germanic peoples, including the Saxons and Angles in Britain, whose naming flourished in many areas. Thus in English place-names, Germanic elements tend to dominate for inhabited places, but mountains and rivers are inclined to be Celtic. Something similar happened on the Continent: a basic syllable something like *rhe-,* from a word meaning to run, turns up as the *Rhine* in Germany, the *Rhone* in France, the *Reno* in Italy, the *Rega* in Spain, and the *Rhye* through which, according to the old song, young folks were " 'cumin' through." Thus we have in England not only the *Avon* running through Stratford, *avon* being a Celtic word for river; we have also *Upper Avon, Lower Avon, East Avon,* and *Avons* in Scotland and Ireland. Three streams are named *Ouse,* a water word, along with *Use,*

Ousel, and *Uouseburn. Est,* also, can mean water. There are *Est* streams in Cumberland, Devon, Donegal, Dumfries, and two each in Forfashire and Edinburghshire, along with the same word in such variant spellings as *Uisge, Wisg, Esky, Ock, Oke,* and dozens more, especially as syllables like *-es-, -wis-,* and *-ees.* A river may have two such names; the *Thames,* presumably from a Celtic word for broad and smooth, is also called *the Broad Isis,* preserving a form of *esk.*

Apparently, the cumulative naming worked like this. A wave of Celts would move south or west and overcome their predecessor Celts. Seeing a river, a newcomer would ask what it was. Conquered peoples tend to detest their conquerors and even to consider them stupid; consequently, the first-wave Celt would be likely to tell the second-wave Celt that the stuff was water, using his own term for H_2O, whether *der, avon, rhe, esk, ouse,* or whatever. The second-wave Celt would accept this designation as a particularizing term and add his own word for water or river to it. Of course all these names piled up and acquired new layers from the Germanic invaders when they came along; *Ouseburn* is made up of *ouse* for running water in Celtic, *bourne* for running water in Old English, and *river* or *creek* or *brook* could now be added to it, making the name river-river-river. Thus streams can be found everywhere in the British Isles with two, three, or more syllables for water or waterlike qualities lurking within their names.

Predictably, very common place-names are those suggesting that somebody lives there. A few Celtic terms survive; Cymric *tre-,* a place, is presumably preserved in *Treves, caer* (fortress) in *Carlyle* and *Carlisle,* and Celtic *baille* (a dwelling) in names like *Balbriggen.* Some borrowed words have crept in; Latin *castrum* appears in words like *Lancaster* and *Doncaster;* the more common form is *chester* as in *Chesterfield, Chesterton, Chesterville, Chester Brook, Chester Hill,* and *Chester* itself. The Latin word for colony appeared with a Celtic term in ancient *Lindum Colum,* now *London,* and other Roman settlements left Latin words like *port* in *Bridgeport, South Port, East Port. Portsmouth* must be both Latin *port* and Old English *mouth.* Minor Germanic elements account for Norse *thwaite* as in *Braithwaite* and Old English *thorp* or *throp* as in *Northrop,* and *stead* (however spelled, including *-sted* and *-stede*) as in *Hampstead, Brested,* and *Grimmsteed.* Many names utilize a term that appears in both Old English and Old Norse with forms like *-by, -bye,* and *-byr;* thus *Appleby* could mean apple orchard or apple farm and *Sotheby* would be the south place. Old

English *burh,* for an enclosed area, survives in names like *Edinburgh, Brattelboro,* and *Edmondsbury.*

Among the most fruitful terms are *ham* and *ton* in various trans-mogrifications. *Ham* in either Old English or Old Norse is our word *home* and the root of our word *hamlet,* a little town, and can represent greater or lesser densities of population. But it is everywhere; in Yorkshire there is *Ham, North Ham, East Ham,* and *West Ham.* There are *Nottinghams, Birminghams, Grahams, Uphams,* and *Greathams* without number. As for *ton,* it is from Old English *tun,* which may mean an inhabited enclosure, but it gets mixed up with *don* from the ancestor of our word *dune,* as is mentioned above, and appears as *-ton, -town, -dun, -don, -doun, -duin,* and many more in *Washington, Charlestown, Huntingdon, Wimbledon,* and *Hunsdowne.*

Terms for homes can pile up. Another of these syllables meaning place or farm is *-ing,* so that names like *Washington* and *Huntington* have two words for a dwelling place, as do dozens of others, including *Hampton* and *Hampstead,* which contain an intrusive /p/, because that is the stop that naturally closes the corresponding nasal /m/. The words mean, in effect, *town-town* or *home-home. Byington* is three words for place, and *Byington Court* is four.

PAPA, MAMA, AND NAME-GIVING

Given names may follow patterns suggested by parental pride or hope, or by family or religious tradition. In Hebrew *Abigail* means father's joy and *Dorothea,* reduced to *Dorothy,* means gift of God. In Latin *Beatrice* is "she that makes happy," and *Florence* means flourishing. In Old English *Ethel* means noble, *Winifred* "friend of peace." Girls got named for flowers (*Rose, Daisy, Lily*), for jewels (*Opal, Ruby, Pearl*); *Margaret* and *Marguerite* mean both pearl and daisy. Boys tended to be named for courage or strength of mind or body; *Andrew* is presumably Greek for strong and manly, *Arnold* Teutonic for strong as an eagle, *Charles* or *Carl* or *Karl* or *Carolus* and the like in many languages mean something like powerful in every way. *Dean* is Latin for the leader of ten soldiers, *Edward* Old English for the guardian of property, and on through the alphabet to *Zebulon,* which means something like princely.

Some names, especially religious names, have been borrowed into many tongues, and reborrowed. *John,* having been spread by both John the Baptist and John the Apostle, provides a prime example. Presumably from Hebrew *yĕhōhānān,* it has sired English *John* and *Jon, Jonathan* (with derivatives like *Johnson, Jonson, Jenkins, Hanson, Jack, Jackson,* etc.), *Jenny, Jan, Jane;* Latin *Johannes, Ioannes;* French *Jean, Jeanne, Jehan;* German *Johan, Hans, Hanson;* Spanish *Juan, Juanita;* Italian *Giovanni, Gianni;* Russian *Ivan;* Portuguese *João;* Welsh *Evan, Evans, Ivins, Ian;* Irish *Sean, Shawn.* The related feminine *Hannah* or *Hanna* in Hebrew accounts for *Ann,* however spelled, and gets into *Joanna.* There are nicknames like *Jacques* and *Jack* and special uses like *John Doe* and *John Hancock.*

Personal naming involves the zeal to call a child "after" somebody, a relative or friend, or a venerated religious or heroic figure. This "naming after" can be complicated. Consider *George.* The word presumably designates a farmer of some sort, being Latin from Greek *georgos* (related to our word *geography*), a worker in the earth, and someone of that name may or may not have been martyred by Diocletian about A.D. 305. Venerated in Oriental churches, he became known to the West during the Crusades for slaying dragons (equated with the devil) and saving maidens. He was a favorite in art and in folk and religious plays. The patron of warriors, he became the commonly recognized patron saint of England, with his cross in the Union Jack and a day in the calendar. The Baroness Dudevant, known as both a novelist and a feminist, took the nom de plume *George Sand* because on St. George's day she had been encouraged to publish under her own name. Six British rulers, and more on the Continent, were named for St. George, along with other worthies like the martyr George of Cappadocia and the humanist George of Trebizond. *George* became a surname.

Thus if a mother names her son *George,* she may be recalling a supposed saint, any of a galaxy of kings, princes, barons, and lords who have taken the name; she may be naming him after the Father of His Country (if she is an American), George Washington, after the great economist Henry George, the statesman David Lloyd George, the poet Stephan George, or even after a famous racing stallion, George Wilkes, or any of the millions of fathers, uncles, cousins, friends, or employers who have been named *George* for any of the churchly, governmental, artistic, or legendary Georges. Presumably all infants now called *George* owe their name to that supposedly once-existent Greek in whose family there must have been a farmer, but the ways in which a boy can now become *George* are innumerable.

NAMING IN A NEW WORLD

As British nomenclature reveals the onomastics of an established community, naming in the United States typifies the practices of a new land. In the mother country everybody was born into a named world; he lived in a named community in a named nation, near a named body of water or a named river running through a named valley, on a named plot of ground, reached by named roads. Even his own name might be predetermined by his saint's day or an ancestor. The New World was in part a new world because it seemed unnamed. Of course it was not; millions of Indians, speaking hundreds of tongues, had named all salient features, named them many times, but most of these titles were now forgotten, and even those still common among the Redmen were mostly unknown to the whites. Thus the American settlement led to a veritable binge of place-naming.

Some old practices continued; places were named for their use or their appearance. *Cape Cod* was a cape where cod could be caught, and *Oyster Bay* an inlet abounding in oysters; there were *Long Islands, Clearwaters,* and *High Tors. Hog Island* in hundreds of pioneer communities provided water-bound pasture where hogs could be left unherded. In the west were *Dry Creeks* in contrast to *Wet Creeks* because in the semidesert creeks go dry in summer; in the South different fauna and flora provided *Alligator Alley, Coconut Grove,* and *Pompano Beach.* Languages made a difference. *Palo Alto* could as well be *Tall Tree* and *Sault Ste. Marie* could be *Mary's Falls,* except that some explorers spoke Spanish and some French. And then, of course, there are Indian words, from *Penobscot,* Maine, to *Snohomish,* Washington, with *Wapsipinnicon* and *Minnehaha* between.

But from the start the New World was self-conscious about names, and new patterns appeared. In the Massachusetts Bay Colony the General Court determined whether *New Marblehead* could be named for old *Marblehead,* and whether the plantation at Musketequid should or should not be given a peace-loving name like *Concord.* More recently, the post office, by declining to deliver mail at an address that duplicates another—and by suggesting names that the office will accept—has influenced thousands of names; the forest service has dealt in names, discreetly expurgating *Squaw's Ass* in favor of *Round Mountain*. Supervisors have named railroad depots by lifting terms from encyclopedias, and city fathers have brought order into street-naming by arranging presidents, colleges, flowers, trees, or what-not in alphabetical order. And now real estate developers bestow lot-selling names; *Bellevues* may have no view and *Woodlawn Terraces* no grass, trees, or elevated ground. Explorers and settlers in the New World have been great "namers-after." During colonial days they tended to name for sovereigns—*Jamestown, Virginia, Charleston, the Carolinas, Georgia, Maryland.* In the Southwest and in Latin America places commemorate religious figures, the Virgin, the saints, even sacred objects and activities, including *Sacramento* and *Vera Cruz* (in Spanish, the sacrament and the true cross).

The New World called also for new generic terms useful in naming. Some have dialectal origins; they were known in British English but either not used in the mother country as place-names or were rare in this sense. *Marsh* is common for wet lands in England and for salt marshes elsewhere, but in the United States the common term for mucky ground is *swamp,* first recorded in this sense by Captain John Smith, who identified swamps in Virginia. The word had been associated with a depression or with sagging; a seventeenth-century anatomy records, if in "a woman with childe the breasts do suddenly fall swampe as we say, then will she abort or miscarry." Similarly, British English has no distinctive term for a rounded, bare-topped mountain, but in the New World *Bald Knob* became so common that the post office had to discourage it. *Prairie* comes from a French word for meadow, but in the New World the word was attached to vast treeless plains, and led to all sorts of variants, the *chocolate* or *mulatto prairies* of Texas, the *trembling prairies* of the southern deltas, and the *door prairies*—what they were is not clear.

New generics include borrowed terms, some occasioned by phenomena not familiar in the British Isles. Perhaps most notable are the terms for great stretches of open country. The *prairies* have been mentioned; there were also *vegas* (Spanish), *bottoms, flats* (mainly seacoasts in England), *plains*—from which might rise flat *buttes* (French) or *mesas* (Spanish for *table*)—in Florida *glades* from which might rise *hammocks* (English *hummock*), and in the West *playas* (Spanish for dry lake-bottom). Mountains were impressive; *sierra* (meaning *saw* in

Spanish) became the name of a range, and *peak* (from French *pic*, a spear) the name of an individual mountain. Lesser hills can be *bluffs* (probably from *bluff land*) and if eroding, *badlands* (translated from French *mauvaises terres*).

An opening in the mountains could be a *pass* (French), a *notch*, or a *gap*. A sharp valley could be a *canyon* or *arroyo* (both Spanish) in the West, a *coulee* in the upper Mississippi (from French), and less precipitous valleys can be *draws*, or in the South, *bayous* (from an Indian language through French), and a broad-bottomed mountain valley can be a *hole*. A small body of water is likely to be a *pond* in New England, an *ojo* (Spanish for *eye*) or a *water hole* in the west, and a *lake* almost anywhere—in England the word is used as a common noun, but not much in older place-names, probably because as a term for a body of standing fresh water it involved a borrowing from Latin. Names for running water show great variety; *kill* from Dutch is restricted to the Hudson River area and a few others, *run* especially in the southeast, sometimes for the area above tidewater; *brook* and *creek* (the latter usually pronounced /krik/ in the Middle West) have limited distributions. *Branch* and *fork*, because they are mainly discoverer's terms, are likely only if the exploration is upstream rather than downstream. Thus such terms are rare on the west slope of the Alleghenies, explored from the east, but common on the west slope of the Sierra Nevadas, mainly explored from the west. The prevalence of vulcanism in the New World led to names including *lava* and *hot springs*. Natural salt in the Ohio Valley has led to *lick, licking,* and *saline* in place-names, not to mention *mahoning*, a Delaware word for a salt-lick.

The settlement of North America so greatly stimulated name-giving for things that compounding has become a characteristic of American English. American varieties of fish, flesh, and fowl—not to mention insects, spiders, and microbes—were enough like the European sorts to encourage hyphenation. Australia has been separated from the Eurasian landmass long enough so that the kangaroo warranted a distinctive name, but the Americas were linked to Asia at Alaska, and may have had links to Europe. Accordingly, American bears are obviously bears, related to polar bears and the European brown bear. They were called bears, but became *grizzly bears, Kodiak bears, cinnamon bears, spectacled bears,* and the like. Still more numerous are the smaller sorts of creatures that subdivide rapidly. For example, one limited sort of bird, known as a flycatcher, is designated with the following terms:

Acadian, Arkansas, Bonaparte's, brown, Canada, Canadian, chattering, crested, dusky, Lawrence's, pewit, red-eyed, scissor-tail(ed), short-legged, small-headed, Townsend, Traill's, white-eyed, yellow-bellied.

Thousands of Americanisms name birds, hundreds name ducks alone. Color-words, terms like *big* and *little,* and *old* and *new* readily compound. Combinations with *red,* from *red Astrachan apple* to *redwood sorrel* fill many pages of any dictionary of Americanisms, and compounds with *black, green,* and *white* would be commensurate. No one has totalled such compounds; they run into tens, perhaps hundreds of thousands.

THE MEANING OF NAMING

To make something of all this, we might start with a map of Spain. The most important river in the south is the *Guadalquivir;* the word makes no sense if we approach it from Gothic—the Goths moved into the peninsula from the north—or Latin, although the Romans were there, nor in Carthaginian or Phoenician, although there were settlers from Carthage and the Levant. But this cannot be an accident, because there are dozens of rivers in southern Spain that start with the syllable *Guad-.* The Moors provide the explanation; for centuries they controlled southern Spain, but never got much into the more mountainous north. In Africa are similar names, although not spelled in the Latin alphabet, among them the common *Wadi-el-Kebir,* meaning big river, from *wadi,* valley or stream, plus *kebir,* great. Nearby in southern Spain are *Guadalcazar,* from *Wadi-l-Kasr,* river of the palace; *Guadalaxara,* river of stones, *Guadalhorra,* river by the cave; *Guadalimar,* red river; *Guadaira,* mill river—the sorts of place-names one finds everywhere, although in Arabic with a local spelling.

Similarly, names beginning with *a-* or *al-* from the Arabic definite article, cluster around the population centers on or near the southern coast—*Alcala, Alhambra, Albuera, Alicant,* hundreds of them; *Almaden,* meaning *the mine,* is common in the southern mountains.

The Arabic *Medina,* meaning *inhabited place,* occurs five times in Spain. Obviously, many Arabic-speaking people lived in certain parts of Spain for a long time. Of course we do not need place-names to tell us that; documents survive, but in no other way except with onomastics can we tell so much about who lived where in Spain and what they did there.

Thus, naming has aided the study of history and archaeology—many a document, even some languages, have been worked out because a name gave a start. The Rosetta Stone could probably have been deciphered without Cleopatra's name in three languages, but the lady helped. Usually onomastics works with other disciplines, but sometimes it supplies almost the only link to the past. In northern France are three towns called *Ham, Hame,* and *Hames.* These words do not suggest Latin, Celtic, or French, tongues one expects to find naming French soil, but as we have seen, *Ham* is common just across the English Channel. A single term might record a random coincidence, but names abound nearby that must be English; *Wimille* makes no sense in French, but just across the Channel in Kent is *Windmill.* So French *Warhem* must be English *Warham, Le Wast* must be the same as *Wast* in several English counties; *Cohen, Cuhem,* and *Cuhen* in northern France probably reflect *Coughan* in Suffolk, across the Channel. *Appegard* is difficult in French, but *Applegarth,* meaning apple orchard, is common in England. *Inghem* seems to mean nothing in French, Celtic, or Latin, but in English it is just one of those combinations of names for a dwelling place *-ing* and *-ham* giving *Ingham,* common in England. That is, there must have been a settlement of Germanic-speaking people in northern France. Were these Angles, Saxons, or Jutes on their way to Britain? Were they English followers of the Black Prince? Did they represent some colonization associated with the religious wars that sent Protestants also to Plymouth Rock? The implications can be argued, but the evidence is mainly from names.

Probably more significant—and certainly more important for this volume—is the impact of naming upon language. This sort of thing must have been happening from the dawn of time: an old word *fahren,* which meant to travel, is preserved as indication of a place where one can go through a river, a *ford.* The place is called the *Ford,* and *Ford* becomes the personal name of people who live there. *John Ford* is a playwright, another by the name a movie director, and *Ford Maddox*

Ford a novelist; a *Ford* named Henry developed a cheap automobile, and now *Ford* is one of the international words. Similarly, *Coke* involves names; it has a complex origin, including the use of *ko-ko* because the *coconut* looked to some Portuguese like a grinning monkey, but it is now perhaps the most widely used Americanism. It must be capitalized when used to designate a beverage in the United States, because it has been copyrighted—names can be worth millions—but an Australian aborigine cannot be sued if he uses the word as a common noun. Only in places like comic strips can one tell when speakers talk in capital letters. So the cycle has been completed, from words to names to new words no longer names. The impact upon vocabulary is incalculable.

4

LANGUAGE
AS ECONOMY

GRAMMAR

Like society, language works by interaction with itself. Theoretically, it need not. We have seen that anything can have a name—animate or inanimate, a movable object or an immovable place, even an idea or a concept having no real existence—and that these names in use may do little more than identify. That, apparently, is much of what the Japanese monkey with his thirty-seven distinguishable cries is mainly doing. Theoretically, he could extend these verbal signs, devising a sign for every conceivable object and for every possible relationship. Monkeys have not, presumably because they could not, and for that matter, neither could we. No doubt a computer could be devised to manipulate the tens of millions of names that would be required, but as yet none has been, and we can scarcely imagine a living input-output device that could remotely approach the brain-competence required for a potentially infinite signal system relying on names only.

That is, a language works—or to put the notion in another way, signals become a language—because users of the signals can show how linguistic bits interact within a system. Or, in the interests of clarity, because language is multifarious and its means seem to be at least plural, we might say that language works by a system of systems. Of these we may conveniently notice two sorts: One concerns what we commonly call words, including names; to these systems we must return. Another sort involves interaction among meaningful bits, including names. Such systems we may call *grammar*.

Before we start asking questions about grammar, let me enter a caveat. I am not saying, and I do not wish to imply, that language began when man first gave names to things and then found ways of combining these names. We know too little about the early growth of language to determine either the antiquity or the relative importance of activities like naming. What we do know is that man has been naming from time immemorial and that naming is the sort of activity one would expect to be early. As for grammar, it has grown with linguistic use, and this growth has been continuous since our earliest evidence. Furthermore, we would expect it to be old; pointing is a sort of grammar, as are loudness of voice and tone. Thus one can scarcely escape the inference that naming and grammar must be very old in language and important in its growth, but for the moment I am concerned only with them as convenient means of thinking about language and what it is. I am not calling them firsts.

With that reservation I return to grammar. Obviously some manifestations that might be called "grammar"—although usually they are not—can be simple, even incidental. If I say the word *pool* you can only guess what I mean, but if I am wearing a pair of wet bathing trunks you are likely to assume I am referring to a body of water, whereas if I am carrying a cue you will surmise I am referring to a game. That is, these nonlinguistic objects, the wet trunks and the cue, imply the working of language to the extent that they suggest a choice among the possible meanings of the name *pool*. If *POOL* is printed on a board in the lobby of a resort hotel, particularly if the board resembles an arrow, the word plus the arrow-sign need no longer be thought of as the name of a physical object. They can now be directions or instructions, the equivalent of a sentence such as "Go in this direction if you want to reach the pool."

Such nonlinguistic contexts for linguistic signs are everywhere. A building bears the sign, *BROWN BODIES:* if sensuous or stimulating music emanates from the building the place may be a torrid night spot, but if the sounds suggest metal being pounded it is probably an automobile body repair shop run by a Mr. Brown. The phrase *Savage Plumbers* could indicate the ferocity with which skilled workmen attack a leaky faucet, but in the instance I know the phrase is the name of a plumbing company operated by a Mr. Savage. *Ford* acquires different sorts of grammar, depending upon whether it appears as an entry in a dictionary, is shouted by a drill sergeant, is molded into a hub cap, or is enamelled on a road sign. Similarly, *Jesus* can be involved in various sorts of grammar depending on many variables, including manners of speaking; its use and meaning would be revealed in part by pitch and volume if the word serves as answer to a theological question, as an appeal in prayer, as an oath, or in instructions issued to a Mexican employee.

That is, grammar can be thought of as a context, in English most obviously as words in context, or elements within words. The context is mainly nothing so obvious as a piece of painted wood in a hotel lobby, but it is there, and it is essential to expression or understanding. Using am I words the of order the change to now were I if (or to use the conventional rather than the reversed order: *If I were now to change the order of the words I am using*) you as a reader would become sharply aware that you and I have something in common that permits me to write and you to comprehend what I am trying to say. What this *something* may be is hard to say; it employs a skill that each of us has acquired, mainly without knowing how or even why. It involves mutual understanding; anything as permeating as the use of language can scarcely be only a skill, even an intellectual skill. It must relate to being human; apparently primates cannot be human without language, and a language is so much the adjunct of humanity that only human beings have ever devised one. Nobody knows where and how, in all these egg-hen, hen-egg doings, grammar appeared and grew, nor has anybody sharply and adequately described it. But for whatever we can make of grammar, language is instinct with it.

GRAMMAR: WHAT IT IS NOT

That is the way I shall try to use the word *grammar,* as a designation of whatever makes language work. The word can be used in other ways—in entirely legitimate ways—but to reduce the confusion I shall avoid certain uses. The word *grammar* can refer to a book or its contents, to an attempt to describe or define the working of a language; this use will be obvious in such titles as *An Elementary Grammar* or *An Advanced Grammar of English.* A common use, it is enshrined in high places; Edward Sapir, one of the great linguists of all time, in the course of pointing out that nobody has ever been able to devise an adequate grammatical statement, observed that "All grammars leak." Obviously, he is here using the word to refer to published works or the contents of them, not to grammar as the working of language. Grammar itself, as the means by which we understand one another, does not leak, or if it does, not much. The grammar itself may leak in a sentence like "The deer had my sympathy." Neither the noun nor the verb indicates how many deer are involved, but only because an old noun has not been incorporated into the Modern English predicative system (contrast: "The deer has my sympathy"; "The bears had my sympathy"). Miscomprehensions of course there are, but usually from my or your failure to use the language well, not from the inadequacy of the language itself. Mainly the book leaks, not the grammar that is the subject of the book. When I must refer to an attempt to describe grammar I shall use a term like a *grammatical statement,* a statement made about grammar, not grammar as the working of language.

Of the other uses of *grammar*—dictionaries commonly recognize a half-dozen or so—one more is common enough to warrant being eliminated. If I were to write in the discussional part of this book, "That guff ain't no good," the publisher's editor would be properly horrified, and would try to get me to revise my terminology. If he were unsuccessful and the sentence should be printed, you would probably be irked and would surely wonder why a reputable publisher issued anything so gauche. Asked why you objected, you might say, "Because it's bad grammar." You would of course be right, but one might notice that *grammar,* in the sense in which I am using the word, is not involved. The language does work that way; you and the editor would be in no doubt about what I meant to say, but for propriety you would feel I should have written, "That thesis is ill-founded," or "Your conclusion is illogical." These sentences would be more revealing for discerning readers than "That guff ain't no good," but for many readers they would be less comprehensible and thus worse. But most objections would not be based on imprecision; the condemnation embodied in the phrase *bad grammar* stems from the conviction that *ain't* is not acceptable usage in serious writing, and that double negatives like *ain't no* are illogical. These are questions of etiquette in language, or propriety; for such matters I shall use the word *usage:* see Chapter 11.

GRAMMAR: HOW NOT TO KNOW
WHAT YOU'RE TALKING ABOUT

So now we are back to *grammar,* where first we might notice that although I have written three paragraphs to distinguish my use of the word, we probably cannot hope that a loose category like "the way language works" will define sharply. Roughly, one can say that all languages have some sort of meaningful units—notably in English, *words*—and means of handling these units, *grammar.* This statement would seem to imply that grammar is structure; indeed, many grammarians have proceeded as though it is only structure, or best understood as structure. And it surely involves structure; a few paragraphs earlier I wrote a clause by reversing the order of the words, that is, by destroying its sequential structure. The passage became gibberish; obviously, the structure had enough to do with the grammar so that with a different sequence the clause became "ungrammatical" in my sense. It had truly "bad grammar"; it could not work as English. On the other hand, you knew the clause was gibberish mainly because it had no meaning. Obviously, meaning also has something to do with grammar.

Similarly, syntax can be involved in grammar, as in a famous phrase noted by the linguist Noam Chomsky, "the shooting of the hunters." The passage can refer to the hunters shooting something or being shot by somebody. Likewise, another Chomskyan sentence is ambiguous because of uncertain syntax; "Flying planes can be dangerous" may have one meaning from the point of view of the pilot, another for the householder who lives near an airport. Even the line between grammar and usage may not be very sharp. In the combination, *the engines stalls,* does the confusion stem from the verb failing to agree in number with the subject (*the engine stalls* or *the engines stall*), from confusing the possessive *engine's* with the plural *engines,* or what? Thus, in more than one sense when we discuss grammar we may not know what we're talking about, but something can be done to categorize it.

If you fear you do not know the rules of grammar, you are partly right and partly wrong. You do know English grammar as a working body of practices—presumably not all of it, but most of it. Otherwise you could not be reading this book nor could you carry on a conversation. Every human being not imbecilic learns at least one grammar, albeit most of it unconsciously. On the other hand, you probably know relatively little grammar consciously enough to formulate it in rules—even though you are formally aware of what I have called usage and could explain why *she doesn't* is acceptable and *she don't* is not. In fact, most people are not aware that there is any such thing as grammar, or if there is, that they ever learned it. They started learning it soon after they were born, as part of their infant mimicry of anything they saw or heard. It was not like breathing, something they knew from birth; nor was it like walking, something they probably would have learned even if they had never seen anybody do it. But they learned it so early that literally they never gave it a thought.

You probably started learning your native grammar as soon as you stopped squalling enough to listen. Your eyes could not yet focus, but your ears did not need to focus—they could work when you were born. You could not see well enough to recognize other members of the family by sight, but you could soon identify them by their hands on you and by the sounds they made. For you, these sounds were not so much the segmental phonemes I was describing in the last chapter, sounds like /b/ or /e/, but what are technically called *suprasegmental phonemes*, the pitch and rhythm of speech, not anything that you would be likely to think of as words or parts of words. Such modulations of voice provide the means through which grammar is expressed in spoken language. Thus, almost from birth you began to learn the machinery of grammar, the rhythms of English sentences, the breath control that makes speech possible; you even practiced these grammatical techniques in your infantile babbling. Thus when, later, you began to learn words, you already had the means you would need to put these words together into grammatical sequences. You were learning how to make language work before you had any words that could be inserted into grammatical patterns.

For this same reason, that most grammar is learned unconsciously, nonliterate peoples have mainly been unaware that there is any such thing as grammar. They are likely to know there is more than one language, or at least that other peoples cannot speak their language. If they know of more than one tongue they will know that different bodies of speech have different words or wordlike clusters. They will know about usage, will find mispronunciations by foreigners funny, and they may believe there is a right and a wrong way to say something, or a good and a bad way. But they are not likely to suspect either that there must be some common fundamental understandings and practices in all language or that each language will have its own collection of deeply based mutual agreements without which it would be unusable.

Thus grammatical statements—*grammar* in the sense of being grammar books—are late in man's long term on earth. Troglodites probably did not while away the tedium of the long nights debating the concordance of verbs; if they did we would have no transcripts, but one doubts they so squandered time. Even in early written works authors *used* language; they did not much deliberate upon it. The Indian Panini wrote an excellent grammar of Sanskrit; Dionysius Thrax and others among the Greeks studied grammar, and Romans picked up the practice from them. But these persons were profound thinkers in great civilizations; even in the Western European tradition grammar was not until recently a matter of much concern except as a device for learning a foreign language like Latin or Greek.

CLASSICAL GRAMMAR BECOMES
UNIVERSAL GRAMMAR

Now we might notice that grammatical thinking was contaminated almost at the source, and the reason is both curious and revealing. First to what happened, later to why it happened. Aristotle was deeply perceptive enough to see that language is so indigenous to man that man himself must be reflected in it. That is, in man's universe there must be something universal in language. Being at heart what we call a college professor, Aristotle examined evidence to derive principles. He studied Greek tragedies to discover the nature of tragedy, Greek lyrics to reveal the nature of lyric poetry. He generalized about communication using the Athenian speech he knew and could not imagine how limited was his sample. Just as he could not include Chinese plays in his theory of tragedy or Eskimo lyrics in his theory of poetry, he could not include the Basque verb system in his study of grammar. Egyptian and Hebrew were nearby, but how could he learn even these languages without books or informants, to say nothing of perfecting the techniques we now believe essential to linguistic research? Greek study of language became mainly a study of local Greek.

Language, especially rhetoric but to a degree grammar, was a Greek specialty and Athens became the fashionable center for what we would call higher education, for grammarians as well as others. Roman grammarians observed what they could scarcely fail to notice—that their native tongue, Latin, closely resembled Greek, especially in its grammar. From this similarity they drew the logical conclusion that grammar was a universal kind of thing, similar everywhere, like life or water, and when Latin grammarians became Christian grammarians they assumed that this unity in grammar was part of the single gift of God when He bestowed language on man. Furthermore, for Christians the assumption that grammar would be best represented in Greek and Latin was plausible enough; the Bible as they knew it was written in Latin and Greek, and Latin, in addition to being the language of the known world, the language of God's church and the medium of His services, was also, they assumed, the language spoken in Heaven, and for that matter in Hell—devils had to be exorcised in Latin, if one hoped to be rid of them. Deities and devils alike, when they appeared in manuscript illuminations, have banners coming out of their mouths —the forerunners of the balloons that appear in modern comic strips— with lettering in Latin.

These classical savants were quite wrong, of course. They had observed closely and they were thinking logically, but they lacked information that was not to be discovered for a millennium or two. They did not know that several thousand years before their day there had lived, in east central Europe, a body of people who were proving to be good emigrators but bad neighbors. These early peoples had a penchant for overrunning everybody they encountered, and they encountered most of the then inhabitants of what is now Europe and parts of Asia. They could neither read nor write, and we do not know what they called themselves; we have named them Proto-Indo-Europeans. We know about them from the dialects they left behind as they traveled, dialects that have grown into modern languages.

Knowledge of them permeates language study, and we must return to them in Chapter 6, but for the moment we need consider only their grammar. They used what we would call sentences, with subjects, verbs, and complements—although not all grammars do. They spoke with words—which not all speakers do, at least not exclusively. They had a verbal system that hinged on time, which they indicated through internal changes within the root of a verb and through endings applied to the root. They had an elaborate case system by which each noun bore as part of its form evidence as to its use in a sentence. These shapes of nouns and verbs, and even of modifiers, could be arranged into elaborate paradigms, working in accordance with what we would call rules.

Thus, when the Roman grammarians observed that Latin paradigms were much like Greek paradigms, they were right as far as they could go, but they could not go far because they did not know their ancestor language, Proto-Indo-European (abbreviated PIE). They could not observe that although Latin paradigms resemble Greek paradigms, they resemble PIE paradigms even more. Nor could the Roman grammarians know that most languages get on without anything that looks much like a Latin paradigm. Latin and Greek paradigms resemble each other not mainly because they embody something universal, but because they have a common ancestor. The two languages have inherited similar paradigms from PIE, and each has changed the grammar in its own way. This is not to say that Greek and Latin grammars had no common ground that represents universal grammar; to that question we must return, but the most notable similarities reflect streams of inheritance from a common ancestor. Accordingly, when the early grammarians studied Latin and Greek—while remaining unaware of the thousands of other languages and dialects known to have thrived on the earth—they were studying only a small fraction of one percent of knowable grammar, obviously an inadequate sample, particularly because it was not chosen scientifically. It was not even a good random sample.

Thus the notion of a universal grammar suffered from a blunder that seemed logical at the time. It suffered even more from an illogical blunder, from the use of the word *grammar* as a sliding middle term, from the same blunder modern purists make when they confuse what I am calling grammar with what I have called usage. Grammar is surely in part universal, but usage obviously is not; it varies with time and place, but if one word, *grammar,* is used both for the working of language and for linguistic etiquette, confusion is easy. Thus in the past a good many somewhat learned persons have been confused, perhaps especially divines, editors, and teachers who knew Latin but knew less about language than they believed they did.

The movement centered in the seventeenth and eighteenth centuries, the time variously called the Enlightenment, the Age of Reason, the

Neo-Classical period, and the like. Philosophers, returning to the classics, and trying to think more clearly than had their predecessors, picked up the notion of Universal Grammar. Some used the idea to good purpose, but some confused grammar as the working of language with grammar as current idiom. They endeavored to purify the English of the day, and they invoked the universe in their support. English was crude, many of them believed, because it had come from Old English, which they termed a most "barbarous jargon." It was usable for serious purposes, they asserted, only because it had been refined on the basis of Latin, although inadequately refined—since "Latin in its purity was never in the Island." They trusted, however, that better Latin could now be used to improve it, and those who declined to be corrected on the Latin model were said to write English that was "barbarous," "vile," "inelegant," and benighted "from the darkness both of Sophistry and Error." That is, English usage (termed "grammar") should follow universal usage, which for practical purposes would be embodied in Latin usage. Even Shakespeare and the Bible were said to be "Lacking in correctness," and less venerated writers fared worse. The religious leader George Fox wrote that anyone who used *you* as a singular, as most people were doing in his day, was an "Ideot and a Fool." In all this, whatever Aristotle meant by Universal Grammar was pretty much forgotten, and with the nineteenth-century study of nonwritten tongues it declined even more. So highly varied are the languages of Asia, Africa, the Americas, and Oceania that students of language became impressed with the diversity in grammar, not with any universality in human speech.

As we have seen, all this grew in part from confusion among definitions of *grammar*. But not all philosophers fell victim to a sliding middle term, and as some modern linguists have pointed out—notably the Noam Chomsky mentioned earlier—one of those least likely to be tripped was the mathematician and philosopher Descartes. His work was largely ignored in his own day and until long thereafter; to see it in perspective we should first review what happened after he was dead and before his ideas were resurrected.

CORRECTNESS, PARSING, AND PHILOLOGY

In view of the great veneration for Latin, and with the nineteenth-century zeal for correctness, especially in the United States, we need not be surprised that Latin parsing was imported also for English. Parsing made sense for Latin. Most words had one of many distinctive endings; a native speaker learned these endings as an American child learns word order, unconsciously, and once he had mastered them he knew how a word worked in a sentence and how it was related to other words. Parsing did not work so well for Modern English, which has few endings.

Undoubtedly, the greatest monument to parsing in English is Goold Brown's *The Grammar of English Grammars*. To see how parsing worked, let us try Brown's method on a simple sentence, "The red brick dwelling slowly fell to pieces." *The* is the definite article; *red* is the name of a color, a noun, since "a noun is the name of any person, place, or thing that can be known or mentioned." The same definition fits *brick*. On the other hand, if *brick* is a noun, *red* may be a preposition, because a preposition is said to be "a word used to express some relation of different things *or* thoughts to each other, and is generally placed before a noun or pronoun." *The* and *brick* are "different things or thoughts, and *red* is involved "in some relation" between them. *Dwelling* we might call a verb, since a verb is "a word that signifies *to be, to act,* or *to be acted upon.*" *Dwelling* is acting; on the other hand, it is the name of an action, and hence it may be a noun, but since it ends in *-ing* it can be a participle, in which case, according to Brown, it can partake of a verb, a noun, or an adjective. *Slowly* can be an adjective, since that part of speech is said to "be added to a noun or pronoun"—and there seem to be plenty of nouns around to which it might be added. An adjective "generally expresses quality," and *slowly* identifies a quality of action. *Fell* gives trouble; Brown recommends consulting a dictionary if the parser is in doubt, and if we look up *fell* in Webster's dictionary, we find that it can be one sort of adjective, either of two sorts of verbs, and either of two sorts of nouns. *To* can be an adverb, since adverbs frequently follow verbs, as in *he came to,* and can modify almost anything but nouns. Or it may be the sign of a verb, since *pieces* may be a verb as in *She pieces the quilt.* Or it may be a noun, and *piece* can be an adjective.

As grammatical analysis, this is of course outrageous. I deliberately used Brown's definitions to get the wrong answers. Brown would never have so analyzed this sentence nor would his pupils—but not through anything they could learn from Brown's parsing. His students would have known at once that *dwelling* is the subject and *fell* the verb, and accordingly they would have sorted much of the sentence into place. They would have had trouble with *fell to pieces*—and so would Brown. Even when one says that *to* is a preposition, we still do not know what is happening in the sentence. In fact, here we face the principal weakness of parsing as a means of dealing with English grammar; it tells too little. Labeling parts of speech is inaccurate; it leads to confusion and blunder, but even if one can properly identify words, we still know very little of what is happening in a sentence.

With the growth of what was called philology during the nineteenth century, grammar fared rather better. Philologists understood that a grammatical statement must describe the grammar of the particular language, and that the grammar of any language can be expected to differ from the grammars of all other languages. Philologists reemphasized such concepts as subjects, predicates, and complements, but as a matter of fact the grammatical statements they devised—although excellent in many ways—sounded rather like descriptions of Latin grammar. These statements, if not as inadequate as Goold Brown's, were cumbersome and limited. They did not suffice even for a simple sentence like that above; if *to pieces* is a prepositional phrase, is it part of the verb, a modifier of the verb, a modifier of the subject, a direct object, or what? None of these answers seems obviously the only right one.

And the philologists failed to exploit at least one major idea—that other approaches to grammar are possible. They knew that all grammars utilize various grammatical devices; in dealing with a grammar a scholar may start with any one of several approaches and hence would derive various sorts of grammatical statements, all different and each valid. That is, there is surely such a thing as the grammar of English; a language will always have a way of working, however complex that way may be, but there is no such thing as "*the* grammar of English," if by *grammar* we mean a grammatical statement. In any final analysis there will be as many grammatical statements as there are grammarians, but even broadly there will be as many sorts of grammatical statements as there are valid approaches to language. Some philologists must have known this, but they did not make much of it. In effect they assumed that if we could ever get one good grammatical statement about English, it would inevitably be the true grammatical statement, the only one worth considering.

This was a notable oversight. Granted that there are units of meaning, and that for economy the utility of these units must be enhanced, there are about three possibilities:

Semantic units can be changed in shape. English uses this device in a pair like *girl, girls* and in a sequence like *sing, sang, sung.*

Units can be put together. Thus in *parked* and *kindness,* new grammatical instruments are coined by adding endings—actually old semantic bits—to *park* and *kind.*

In reality, grammatical shapes described in (1) above have mostly come about in this way, by combining previous shapes, so that for practical purposes (1) and (2) can be thought of as one.

Units can be kept apart. Grammar is generated by the way three units are ordered in *Man the ship* and *Ship the man.*

That is, speaking broadly and in light of what we know of the history of language, we can say that to reveal grammar we can put semantic units together or we can keep them apart. When we do either, we can put various sorts of shapes together in various ways, and we can also keep them apart in various ways and for various ends. On the whole, the way in which linguistic bits are combined is fairly obvious, once one knows the history of linguistic shapes; they can be put together in relatively few ways. Keeping units apart can be much subtler and harder to describe. Thus much of the recent grammatical thinking has provided new approaches to studying analysis as a grammatical device, and analysis, as we have seen, is central in Modern English grammar.

STRUCTURE BEGAT GRAMMAR AND GRAMMAR BEGAT STRUCTURE

Among the first of the new approaches to attract wide attention was *structural linguistics.* Structuralists found the statement by the philologists unscientific; it was not objective because it confused meaning and function and because neither was measurable. And without measurement, science becomes impossible. They observed that, on the contrary, structure is measurable; speech is inevitably a linear sequence, and in language linearity is embodied in sound. Nobody speaks two words at once. The structuralists utilized the idea of the phoneme as a working unit of sound and found that they could take any body of language and, by cutting it repeatedly into its *immediate constituents,* they could reduce each sentence to a series of phonemes. For example, they would say that "The red brick dwelling fell slowly to pieces" is made up of two immediate constituents, *The red brick dwelling* and *fell slowly to pieces.* Thereafter, they would make an immediate constituent cut (called an IC cut) before *fell,* and would continue making IC cuts until only phonemes remained. A diagram would look something like this:

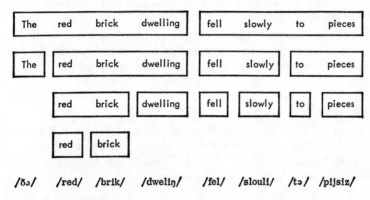

/ðə/   /red/   /brik/   /dwelin̪/   /fel/   /slouli/   /tə/   /pijsiz/

Conventions differed among structuralists, but this diagram suggests the idea. It concerns only what we have called segmental phonemes. Structuralists recognized, however, that oral language uses sound patterns that extend beyond these segmental phonemes, and that such sound patterns are implied in written language. Accordingly, they broke sound patterns into pitch (highness or lowness of tone), stress (loudness and degree of tenseness), and juncture (pauses and all that go with these pauses). That is, in the sentence above, *pieces* would be accompanied by terminal juncture, which can be defined roughly as whatever a native speaker does to close a declarative sentence.

This approach was a sensation. It was more nearly objective than any previous grammatical statement. It revolutionized the study and teaching of unwritten languages, and it was variously used, from infancy on, to teach the native language to the native speakers. But there were skeptics—grammar is one of those pursuits that seem to breed skepticism. Adverse critics objected that after structural linguists had done their best, we still did not know much of what is happening in a sentence. The structuralists countered that their study was as yet in its infancy; in language there must be surface grammar, what we can see and hear, but there must also be deep grammar, the very heart of language. As yet they could study only surface grammar because they were being scientific, telling what truth they knew but telling no fibs about anything that, for the time being, they could not know. They were sure, however, that the more they penetrated into structure the better the questions they could ask, until eventually they would know everything about language. Someday they would be able to ask objective questions about such seeming imponderables as meaning; but meanwhile, first things first.

The structuralist monopoly of linguistic revolutions did not last long. Structural linguistics grew in complexity without growing much in adequacy, and soon another flock of ideas attracted such powerful adherence that publishing structuralists—in the limited sense in which I have been using the term *structuralist* here—are now almost as rare as philologists or followers of Goold Brown, although all modern grammarians make some use of structuralist approaches. The second phase of the twentieth-century grammatical revolution stemmed notably from an ingenious generator of ideas, Noam Chomsky, professor at Massachusetts Instititute of Technology.

MORE NEW LOOKS AT GRAMMAR

Among the basic observations Chomsky shared with some others was this: Previous grammarians, at least those who tried to do their own thinking instead of relying on earlier precepts, had worked with language already in existence. They had examined written language, or oral language already recorded, or made-up language that could be conceived as having been spoken. But Chomsky called attention to another source of grammatical knowledge. Native speakers of a language have a working knowledge of the grammar. They must understand the working of the language because they comprehend sentences they have never heard before, and can themselves generate sentences. That is, the grammar of a language can be discovered by studying the speech practices of competent users of the language, who have a grammatical sense, however they got it. With that, *generative grammar* was born, a grammatical statement that rests upon the competence of speakers to generate sentences.

This idea produced echoes. Chomsky himself, being well-grounded in mathematics, saw it as revealing mathematics-like rules. If one uses the symbol *S* for sentence, the symbol *NP* (noun phrase) for a subject and all that goes with it, *VP* (verb phrase) for the verb and what goes with it, and the symbol → as meaning "can be written as," then for a simple sentence we have *S* → *NP* plus *VP*. That is, a basic rule, familiar to all speakers of English, says that a sentence can be made of a subject and some observation about that subject. The user of a language will have a working knowledge of all sorts of combinations and their values, what we may call *phrase-structure rules,* and thus Chomsky would analyze the sentence above about as follows:

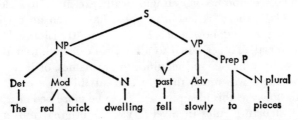

With such branching-tree diagrams generative grammarians can picture a simple sentence, and parts of it can be analyzed with more detailed diagrams.

This sort of approach is usually called *transformational grammar,* although the term is a misnomer if one carries the analysis no farther than this. The diagram above obviously represents a surface approach to grammar, but Chomsky is no man to stop at surfaces. His statement, he feels, provides an insight into deep structure, to Descartes' Universal Grammar, which must embody universals back of all modern language. In other words, he would say that the sentence above, and all other sentences that can be composed in Modern English or any other surviving language, are *transforms* of a way of thinking, even of a structure in Universal Grammar.

In this he cannot be entirely wrong. Human minds being what they are, men must always have been saying "Somebody—did—something; this—is—a certain sort of object; this thing—has—a known quality; I —want (or do not want)—that." That is, needs to use language, and accordingly some uses of language, are universal, and modern statements of the same sort must be to a degree modern versions of these old expressions. And if we do not press the similarity too closely, the modern expression must be a *transform* of the earlier expression. Similarly, as there must have been a way to say, "Cain killed Abel," there must likewise have been a way to say, "Cain did not kill Abel," to ask "Did Cain kill Abel?" and to throw statements into the passive voice and to indicate uncertainty, as in "Abel may have been killed by Cain." These can be thought of as transforms—transformationalists have not agreed on these terms—and there would be many transforms for each; the question could appear, "Cain killed Abel, didn't he?" "Was not Cain Abel's murderer?" "How can we escape the conclusion that Abel was murdered and Cain did it?"—on and on.

Here the discussion becomes linguistically exciting. How closely does "Did Cain kill Abel?" reflect what must have been an earlier grammatical structure and how much has it been "transformed" from an earlier universal? To get down to a case, we can note that there must always have been names and modification of names, or if not "always" as early as there was much thought and anything we could call language. But how was this idea phrased? or to be more pedantic, what are the phrase-structure rules involved? Was the original universal something like *His head is hard* or was the early structure *hard head,* which could then be transformed into a predication about a head or to any of the other structures by which a name and a modifier can be brought together? Likewise, the tendency to simplify language by leaving things out or by implying them must have been universal. For example, pronouns are so obviously economical and are so widespread in language that they must rest upon some universal practice. Consider the following sentences: "My grandfather drank whisky as though it was spring water. He was always drunk." Here the pronoun *he* involves all that we know about the man; that he was the grandfather of the speaker and that he drank straight whisky need not be repeated; the information is all implied in *he,* but the rules that permit *he* to work in this economical way are many and somewhat rigid. Of that we may be sure, even though we do not know enough of Universal Grammar to say what these rules were.

Thus transformational grammar has revived the interest in Universal Grammar although it has not as yet described much of what that grammar must have been. Many transformationalists rely especially on the following sorts of sentences, which have sometimes been called *kernel sentences:*

I wonder (subject, intransitive verb, no complement).

Cain killed Abel (subject, transitive verb, object).

Cain was Abel's brother (subject, copulative verb, complement the equivalent of the subject).

Cain was angry (subject, copulative verb, modifier of subject).

Cain went away (subject, verb, adverb of place).

Presumably, with a few such predications, those that represent inevitable working of the human mind, all grammatical structures can be derived. This is not to say that only grammar can be universal. There must also be something universal about pronunciation; all known languages have both consonants and vowels, and we have seen that these tend to fall into patterns, and Chomsky is among those who have endeavored to show that there are universal patterns in stress. We have already noticed that naming must have something universal about it, and there are no doubt other universals in vocabulary, animate as against inanimate, number, abstract as against concrete, sex, and the like.

Meanwhile, the whole approach is providing refreshing insights. Consider two expressions noticed earlier as ambiguous: *flying planes can be dangerous* and *the shooting of the hunters.* Each sequence has at least two meanings, partly because some of the words have various uses. *Flying* can suggest the action of directing an airplane in flight or it can distinguish planes in the air from those on the ground, but mainly the meanings differ because the syntax is different. That is, two interpretations of the same words reflect different structures in Universal Grammar or structures that have survived through different transformations and have then by accident fallen together in Modern English. This sort of coincidence is inevitable when large numbers of items are involved; the *ear* that means an organ of hearing and the *ear* that means corn on the cob are different words. They had different origins and were long distinct, but through phonetic change they are now spelled and pronounced alike. Something similar presumably happened in *the shooting of the hunters,* although the explanation is provided by the transformations from Universal Grammar.

Generation has become involved, also, in several other sorts of grammatical statements, of which the most widely useful to date can be called *string grammar* or *slot-and-filler grammar*. For example, we know that many English sentences include a subject, verb, and complement; let us think of a sentence as generated by filling such slots:

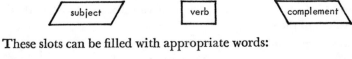

These slots can be filled with appropriate words:

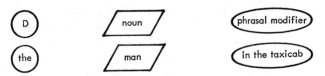

Obviously, these slots could be filled with other words, *Hepsibah appears frumpy, Chimps are friendly,* but in most contexts neither *Frances* nor *gorgeous* could fill the rectangular slot. *Looks* could appear in any of the three—although with other uses and hence probably not the same word—as in "A girl's looks may get her a job," "They gave me dirty looks." And any of the slots could be vacant, as two are in the sentence, "Look!" Each of the slots could have a pattern of slots within it; if the sentence is "The man in the taxicab was staring at me," there would be a series of slots within each major slot. The first could be:

Once one starts thinking of grammar as slots within slots, the system expands without devising new figures for each grammatical use, a device of which particular use is made in a variant called *sector analysis*. As a matter of fact, the system does not solve much; we might be uncertain as to whether the *at* of *at me* should be part of the verb *was staring at* or whether it introduces a phrase telling where the man was staring, but that is only to repeat an earlier observation that grammar is slippery stuff and all grammatical statements leak.

An intriguing approach, essentially a slot-and-filler attempt, is called *tagmemics. Tagmeme* is a coined word meaning something like *hunk,* so that tagmemics could be called grammar by hunks. By this approach, the filler of a slot, a tagmeme, is more than a word; it includes a word or words, but it includes all that goes with the locution, including pronunciation and meaning. The approach utilizes an idea, borrowed from physics, that every segment can be considered, and must be treated, in three ways simultaneously: (1) as particle, (2) as wave, and (3) as field. That is, a bit of language must be treated (1) as itself, (2) in its relations to other particles, as movement, and (3) as part of the whole working of the language. Tagmemics has been successfully used by its inventor, Kenneth L. Pike of the University of Michigan, to deal with oral languages, but at this writing it is not widely used to teach English to native speakers.

Another generative statement, *categorical grammar,* although it was devised to describe English, has found its most ardent devotees on the Continent. The categories are *primary, secondary,* and *tertiary.* What are commonly called subjects are primary; both verbs and adjectives rely upon them and are thus secondary. Adverbial words and structures, along with many particles, are tertiary.

Stratificational grammar opens up tantalizing insights. The brain-child of Sydney M. Lamb of Yale University, it stems from the thinking of the Dane, Louis Hjelmslev, and as its name suggests, treats language by levels. Lamb plumbs below most grammatical concepts, and describes language as upward or downward movement, as co-ordinating or discriminating (that is, *and* or *or*), and as *ordered* or *unordered.* Thus he works with concepts like *upward ordered and* and *downward unordered or;* he plots relationships through diagrams relying on nodes. Adverse critics of the approach have called it philosophically dubious and largely inapplicable; its supporters say it tells more about how language works than can any other analysis as yet proposed. As for Lamb himself, he is a careful scholar who insists that his system requires both checking and refining, but he believes it can be simplified and applied. At the moment his followers are more devoted than numerous.

GRAMMAR: BACK TO MEANING

Now one more approach. Throughout all this confusion as to how grammar can be described, many thoughtful people have refused to ignore the central fact that language is concerned with meaning. Language exists to express and communicate meaning. Of course such a statement requires a broad definition of "meaning"; language can be used to please and delight as an art, it can be used as a social device to promote one's vanity or to while away the time. But dealing with meaning is overwhelmingly the purpose of language, and meaning lies back of language even in aberrant uses, as when a person gains emotional satisfaction from talking with himself. Language may be used for no communication whatever; the sentence "the quick brown fox jumps over the lazy dog" has probably never served to report a happening; it is used in aligning typewriter keys. But if it did not seem to have meaning repairmen would probably not use it. Thus many scholars have stubbornly believed that, because meaning is the essence and purpose of language, it must be central in grammar and should be central in a grammatical statement. They have felt that a grammatical description based on meaning has to be possible; it would not provide the only valid grammatical statement, and it might not be the most nearly scientific, but it could be the most useful, and it should be attempted, if anyone can find a way. Few could; if grammar thought of as sound is slippery, grammar thought of as unmeasurable meaning is much more slippery.

Recently we have had a good attempt. Wallace L. Chafe of the University of California has tried to put new grammatical thought together in *Meaning and the Structure of Language* (1970). He has profited from the structuralists and their insights, from the Chomskyan school and others, but he grounds his statement firmly on meaning, and with meaning he can make as much of transformations and Universal Grammar as Chomsky does with syntax. He recognizes that meaning cannot be objectively defined, but he notices that aspects of meaning can be identified and that relatively determinable components of meaning do become involved in grammar. Users of Universal Grammar must have needed ways to distinguish between animate and inanimate, between male and female, between specific and generic uses. Not only did a person have to say, "Cain murdered Abel," in which the idea of murder is embodied in a specific act, but one had also to say, "Cain is a murderer," in which the generic replaces the particular. And this sort of distinction requires different sorts of syntax—that is, the meaning, not the syntax pattern, determines the grammar, however much syntax may become the instrument of grammar.

Similarly, a sentence can be looked at as various sorts of meaning. Here the main distinction is between what Chafe calls *old* and *new*.

Every sentence must have something old or it becomes incomprehensible; it should have something new if there is to be any reason for the existence of the sentence. In the assertion, "Cain killed Abel," the idea in *Cain* is old in Chafe's sense. Cain may have been under discussion; if not, he is known, and hence is "old" in that some knowledge common to the speaker and the hearer identifies Cain as the "subject." Subjects generally are "old." What we presumably do not know when the sentence starts is what is new, that Cain *killed Abel*. That is, the fact that something is new accounts for the sentence, which in turn accounts for the phonetics, syntax, and anything else that may be needed.

So goes the search for a better grammatical statement as I finish this chapter. *Grammar,* long a term associated with dullness and pedantry, now implies exciting stuff, at once a sport and a battleground, intellectual fun.

5

LANGUAGE
AS THE FINDING OF MINDS

WORDS

Words are like gods, at least in this, that nobody has proved they exist, but they are widely accepted as the means of creation. However one defines *god,* as a benevolent gentleman with whiskers, the order behind solar energy, or something between, the creation of the universe is usually attributed to some superhuman power. The universe is here, as we know by living in it, and the creation presumes a creator. But we also create. We generate sentences, usually hundreds of them every day of our lives, and we shape understandings of such sentences. We develop ideas that we embody in statements of belief, and we enshrine these in language so that they stand, some more durably than the rock-ribbed earth. We have molded language into works of art, plays like *Hamlet,* novels like *War and Peace,* lyrics like Burns' songs, shining things where before was nothing. And these seem to be made of words.

To a degree they are, although less so than may appear. As you read, you see a string of printed symbols running in lines across the page. You are more or less aware of these words and of the ideas that rise in your mind. The words accumulate and the ideas appear; the ready inference is that the meaning comes from the words. We have seen, however, that meaning is more complex than this. The words *red* and *brick* appeared as names of things as long as we considered them separately, but they became modifiers of another object, *dwelling*, as soon as these words worked in phrase structure. We saw that we know how to choose the proper meaning of a word only when we know how the word works in its surroundings, that *fell* could have meanings as varied as *toppled, fearsome,* and *animal skin,* depending upon its phrasal associations. Furthermore, we did not know what was happening until we could distinguish the "old" from the "new," until we knew what is the subject and what is the predication about the subject. If *SHIP FLOUNDERS* is a telegram to a seafood dealer, the message probably is an order for fish, but if the words appear in a newspaper headline, they may concern a disaster at sea. Of course a single word can be a sentence, as in "Fire!" but not because *fire* alone would tell so much. *Fire!* as a shout suggests predication because it implies that somebody needs to be saved from a fire, or that somebody is calling for help to put out a fire. That is, we might have concluded, although we did not, that as far as communication is concerned, the sentence is the most important linguistic unit.

MEANING AS A COMPLEX

Even in meaning, words are part of an elaborate set. If you will glance at the first paragraph in this chapter you will find I wrote the sentence, "But we also create." Although I trust this sentence was clear in context, it is unclear out of context. What does *but* mean? It implies a contrast, but what is contrasted to what and why? Who are *we* —you and I—a body of scholars engaged in a common pursuit, all mankind, or what? What does *also* mean, that *we* and somebody else create or that *we* do something besides create? And even *create* is not clear; in fact it is deliberately intended to have at least two meanings. In short, meaning is so interreliant among the sentences of a paragraph that usually a predication can have its intended import only in relation to other sentences. Less obviously, paragraphs rely upon one another for the meaning of each.

But if the word is not the largest unit of meaning, neither is it the smallest. Take the last word in the previous sentence, *smallest.* It is made up of two working parts, *small* and *-est.* The first can function by itself; the second cannot, but it has semantic use, that whatever is true by the preceding unit is true to the highest degree. That is, both *small* and -*est* are units of form having meaningful use, whence they are called *morphemes*, *small* being a free morpheme because it can function by itself, -*est* being a *bound morpheme* because it can work only if attached to some other unit. Thus *small* is one word and one morpheme, whereas *smallest* is one word but two morphemes. Meaning is likely to be distributed pretty unevenly over units of various size, from the paragraph down to the morpheme, and the word is only one of these units. In fact, if we had a device—we might call it a "meaning-meter"—that would measure the degree of meaning generated by a linguistic unit, we might get a graph something like this:

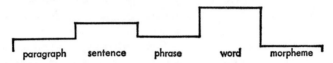

Such a graph has no validity; we do not know how to measure meaning, but it may suggest that although words have meanings of themselves, they are not alone. They are part of a complex that stimulates us to generate meaning as we look or listen.

In fact, some students of language prefer not to use the term *word* at all. Having no definitive use, it cannot be defined with any accuracy; linguistic shapes cannot even be certainly recognized as words. Consider the verb *to be*. It exists in such shapes as *am, is, are, was, were, been, being,* and the like. It comes from three unrelated words, *beon* and *wesan* in Old English, and something related to Sanskrit *asmi*. It has a variety of uses; in "Whatever is, is right," the first *is* means something like *exists*, and the second is a copula almost without meaning. In sentences like "He is skiing," *is* can be described as either a copula or an auxiliary. Most dictionaries, however, treat *be* and all its forms as one word, although it is not one thing in origin, shape, sound, grammar, or meaning. On the other hand, *bushy* and *bosky* are counted as two words, although they have a common origin, essentially the same meaning and grammar, and differ only slightly in pronunciation. Why is *courtroom* one word and *post office* two? *Inasmuch* can also be spelled *in as much; cannot* and *can not* are equally acceptable. Obviously, the question of being a word is complicated. Lexicographers have had to recognize that they cannot put sure limits to words, that they can hope only to produce usable dictionaries. This they do by devising orderly means of putting entries into practical alphabetical sequences. They have labored to be consistent and have devised work-able agreements, but anyone can demonstrate that these agreements cannot be objectively applied. No two dictionaries have the same word list, and the volume that includes only two entries for *fast* may be as authoritative as the dictionary that distinguishes eight or ten.

WORDS AS COUNTERS OF MEANING

Futhermore, languages without words are theoretically possible—although as far as I know, no such language has been discovered—and some languages use relatively few words. English, as we have seen, uses linguistic units having at least one free morpheme; many compounds like *handbook* have two, and some, like *jack-of-all-trades* have more. Like most languages, English has developed free morphemes and is still growing them, because they are economical both for meaning and structure. Some words are in effect made of only bound morphemes; consider words like liter*ate,* literat*ure,* liter*ary,* liter*al,* and *al*liter*ative.* Such combinations are usually considered only as independent words, but they approach a series of bound morphemes. The sequence *-liter-* comes from Latin *litera,* meaning a letter; thus it was formerly a free morpheme, and now it is not anything, having no definable meaning, but it can be used in combination with bound morphemes, as in *al*-liter-*a-tion.* Obviously, the principle could be extended; we might have units usable as subjects and others usable as verbs, although they could work only in combination, never alone, just as *-est, -ary,* and *-ure* cannot appear alone. In fact there are such languages; they include many of the American Indian tongues. In such speech a sentence may be a cluster of syllables, most of which or none of which can be used except with other syllables. Such languages are sometimes called *deriva-tional* or *polysynthetic* because of the various ways in which a sentence can be synthesized, or *incorporating* because the subject may be in-corporated into the verb, the verb into the object, and the like. In certain American Indian languages the subject and verb are both incorporated into the object; thus syllables which mean "Man over there hit," would be the equivalent of Modern English "Somebody hit that man over there."

Users of Modern English, however, find the concept of the word handy. Christians believe that "in the beginning was the word," whatever *word* means in that context, and we quote Browning exclaiming, "What so wild as words are!" But nobody gets into dictionaries of quotations by asking "What so nonexistent as words are?" Words seem to be very existent; we believe we speak them and write them; there they are, identified in the dictionary. Most users of English are much aware of words, almost oblivious of grammar, except insofar as it is usage, and have never heard of morphemes. Thus the name *words* —it is two morphemes, the free morpheme /wərd/ and the bound morpheme /z/ meaning plural—is a good term to work with if not a good term to define with. I shall use it henceforth just as though I know what it means.

As counters of meaning, words partake of a curious duality; in part they rely upon a referent, in part they exist in us and take their growth from us. Most words refer to something; *Gwendolyn* refers to a particular girl, and even *girl* refers to a particular sort of object not readily mistaken for an oyster or a chemical formula. Here we have something rare in language, a one-for-one equivalent. Every use of a word can have a referent, although the referent may serve for more than one use of more than one word, and the referent will be the same for everybody, granted familiarity with the language and the object. I may not know what nickel is or what symbol stands for it, but once I do know, I will infallibly associate the two with each other, and so will anybody who knows chemistry. A word can have more than one referent because it can have more than one use; a nickel may be made from nickel, but it is a piece of money and hence the word has at least two referents, one an element, one a coin.

But designating the referent is only a relatively small part of all a word can do, and here we might observe another curious duality: meaning shifts with the speaker or writer, with the hearer or reader. Except for its referent, a word has nothing objectively measurable in meaning, and the meaning we experience for it lives within us and is obtainable from us. When one uses a word like *nickel* he expects it to do something, and when another person encounters the word it will do something, although never just what the speaker or writer intended. Partly the word will have a meaning because of the way each of us as individuals has lived with the word; and this particularity, grounded in the individuality of the user of language, is supplemented by the occasion. A speaker never means quite the same thing in any two uses of a word, nor will the word have quite the same impact with any two auditors or in any two sets of circumstances. Thus every use of a word is unique, unique in what the user expects it to do, unique also in what a recipient makes of it.

Words grow variously in each of us. The other day I reassured someone, saying, "I don't want this to cost you a nickel." I meant to say I did not want the venture to cost him anything, and unconsciously I used the word *nickel* to suggest the smallest amount of money worthy of consideration. I now recall that as a child I placed a different value on this word. We had very little cash in our household, but a block away was a store where a nickel—if one could ever amass such a treasury as five cents—would buy a bag of candy so huge that I dreamed about it. That is, what the word *nickel* means for me has changed with my lifetime, from great wealth and even a sort of ideal to the embodiment of something trivial. And on the whole *nickel* is not a word that does much for people, nothing like *mother* or *Old Glory*.

Or consider the word *dame;* when applied as a title to Dame Edith Sitwell it connotes something quite different from its meaning for the sex-starved GI's in *South Pacific,* who were convinced there "is nothing like a dame." No doubt these young men had liked girls back in the States, and they would like girls again when they were discharged, but these pleasures would differ from one another and both would differ from the hunger they had known when dumped on a remote island. Even the emotional impact of *mother* is changing, now people have become aware that mothers can do their offspring deep psychological damage and may be helping to overpopulate the globe.

Most meaning, on the other hand, is remarkably standard, as though all speakers had subscribed to an unwritten linguistic contract as to what individual words are good for. Words come from various sources and are constantly changing, and yet most users of a language will feel most of the time that they know what words mean. Obviously, the means by which words are generated and controlled must be complex and subtle.

THE MEANS OF MEANING

Among the means of meaning, some trends are obvious enough. Once we have, by our language-wide contract, agreed that a given metallic element will be known as nickel, some meaning of the term follows readily. We know that nickel has an atomic weight of 58.71, that it boils at 2730° Centigrade, and the like. All this has been worked out and recorded, so that we have a ready basis for some agreement about the meaning of the word that names an element. Similarly, for the word *mother*, we know about parturition, and that a female is involved. Thus, if speakers of English have in essence agreed that a female by giving birth becomes a mother, we know something of what the word means. Thus a word can be a handle for a known body of meaning.

To see how some other meanings develop, we might look more closely at this word *mother*. It presumably comes from a form like *mater*, being made up of a baby's babbling plus the ending *-ter*, which meant a relative. Thus the word identifies the member of a family concerned with the babbler. By an early extension of meaning, females that accounted for birth but were not associated with babblers—cows and mares, for example—were called mothers, and some females had only to lay an egg to acquire the name, once the egg was hatched. This is a common intellectual phenomenon; we call it generalization. A woman who has given birth is called a mother; by extension, any act that gives birth or provides for birth is associated with being a mother. The same principle can be observed in other meanings; a mother looks after a child, so that we can say "she became a mother to her orphaned nephew," or "Romulus and Remus were supposedly mothered by a wolf."

Such developments appear everywhere, and they can push generalization very far. A word may grow so general that it refers to nothing so specific as a referent; we might adopt a term used by the English linguist Simeon Potter, and say it has a sphere of reference. Consider the word *truth;* it has no referent so sharply defined that we can see or hear or smell it and thus point to it, but it has a sphere of reference in the sense that it suggests something other than untruth. But it has a specific origin; it comes from OE *treow,* meaning a tree. Presumably the idea was that a "treow" person stood firmly as a tree, which before the day of stump-pullers and bulldozers was about as firm as you could get. Then the word generalized further to something worth being true to.

But if generalization accounts for meanings, we should expect the opposite mental device, specialization, to have uses, and it does. The administrator of a religious foundation can be called a *mother superior.* *Mother wit,* the *mother country,* and *mother nature* are all specializations from the general concept of *mother,* and *Mother of God,* although it is a personal name, is also a specialization. Some meaning may grow from more limited associations, such as cause and effect. A *mother's mark* was a birthmark, presumably caused by the woman. The womb, the means of becoming a mother, was formerly called the *mother;* as a sixteenth-century anatomist put it, "These thre woordes, the matrix, the mother, and the wombe do sygnyfie but one thyng." Lavender was recommended for "diseases of the mother." Probably as extensions of this meaning, two structures in the brain were formerly called the *hard mother* and the *soft* or *gentle mother,* the first as the translation of the Latin *mater dura,* intended no doubt to mean no more than *hard matrix,* but translatable as *hard mother.*

A mother's conduct was fruitful in words through figures of speech. A *mother stone* is the matrix from which a jewel is extracted as though it were a child from the womb, and the *mother-of-pearl* oyster involves the same figure. Much figurative terminology is so mixed with such mental processes as generalization and transfer that new meanings relying on only one sort of semantic growth are hard to find. For example, a very prolific vein of ore in Mexico was called *Veta Madre,* perhaps because it was named for the Virgin, the *mother-maid,* or because it seemed to brood over many lesser veins, or because it was continually productive, and so on. By translation and comparison, the great quartz vein of California was called the *mother lode,* and when oil was discovered in quantity in Oklahoma the oil field was referred to as "a mother lode of black gold." Meanwhile, snowing was said to come from *Mother Carey* plucking her goose or her chickens, although the term *Mother Carey* was probably a folk etymology from *madre cara,* meaning dear mother. Such figurative uses can develop very rapidly; a few years ago the leading Russian and the president of the United States conferred personally in order that discussion could take place "at the highest level." Probably humorously, this was referred to as a "meeting at the summit," and cartoonists portrayed leaders at such *summit meetings* sitting on mountain tops. Now, lesser diplomats confer in what are called *foothill meetings.* The means of meaning become commingled and obscured as words grow.

SYMBOLS AND SENSE

Notably, words can be studied as symbols. To observe symbolic workings, we might try to distinguish symbols from signs. Beside a highway you may see a metal plate with the following legend: U.S. 8 SOUTH. This is not a symbol. It does not mean the United States, or the cube of the number 2, or the South. It is a sign; it is a direction, telling you which way you are going and on what road. Similarly, a ring around the moon is not a symbol; we may say "It means rain," but it does not "mean" anything. A ring around the moon may be a sign that there will be rain, but a circle within a circle does not mean water falling in natural droplets. A ring on a woman's third finger on the left hand, however, is a symbol in American society; it means that the wearer has a marital arrangement. If the ring has a jewel in it, it is likely to mean that the woman is engaged; if the ring is a plain or engraved band, it probably is her way of saying she is married.

Roughly, a sign that is only a sign does not have meaning; a sign that is also a symbol does have meaning. One might notice, also, that a sign is relatively fixed; it has little power of growth. A roadsign that says, WASHINGTON 40 MILES, can indicate the distance to the city and that is about all it can do. That is what it did yesterday, and what it will do tomorrow. But *Washington* as a symbol can grow in use and meaning. The word is a symbol for a great city; it has become a symbol for the United States, for American foreign policy, for federal bureaucracy, even for crime in the streets. Conceivably *Washington* might become a symbol for solving racial problems, and if the city is obliterated in an atomic war the word could become a symbol for destruction. Given the appropriate circumstances, the term *Washington* might become a symbol for almost anything. That is, a symbol is something concrete and specific that becomes the vehicle for meaning beyond that implied in its literal use; a workman's protective head-covering is indeed a hard hat, but a *hardhat* is a person who wears such headgear, and at this writing the word has lately become a symbol for the politically conservative element among labor.

All words are symbols, most of them in at least two ways. We may start with a string of letters like *h-a-r-d-h-a-t*, with the sound /hɑrd-hæt/, with the equivalent of these in any other language, a gesture in sign language, the dots and dashes of the Morse code, or whatever.

These are signs but can become symbols for the word *hardhat*. The word then becomes a second sort of symbol, at a minimum a symbol for a very resistant helmet. Some words develop only one symbolic use; words like *endopeptidase*, which refers to an enzyme known only to specialists, are unlikely to grow much symbolically, but common words all have many uses and many symbolic overtones.

In dealing with words as symbols we are approaching what language is and what makes human beings human. Man has symbol-sense, and not many creatures do. A dog, shown a photograph of his master, will treat it as he would any other small, thin rectangle; there is likely to be no bark of recognition, no sudden wagging of the tail. To him a photograph is not a symbol. A child, on the other hand, commands symbols very early; I noticed that my granddaughter, as soon as she had the word *fishy*, at the age of fourteen or fifteen months, started applying the term to trout for dinner, to a picture of a fish in a magazine, to a piece of jewelry in the form of a fish, and to an ashtray with a fish motif. Philosophers have suggested that only with symbol was primitive man able to order the multitudinous facts of his mysterious world. Without symbol he probably could never have devised language or learned to think enough so that he could civilize himself. Here one might recall that Washoe could command symbol; we can plausibly guess that without a symbol-sense she never could have learned to use language, and that only those creatures capable of symbolic concepts can ever go far in linguistic communication.

However that may be, we apparently have enough evidence for this statement: *Many words mean what they do because they reflect the way human minds work.* The meaning, of course, is not in the words; the meaning is in us, and if I may repeat a figure I have used elsewhere, I might call a word a ladle with which we dip up meaning. But when we dip, we dip into ourselves. Partly, of course, words reflect the kind of lives we live—if there was no war we would have no military terms. Theological words died by the thousand when theological arguments declined. But granted we have need for words because of what we do and the thoughts we think, we can grow meaning mainly through the working of the mind. We use our symbol-sense, our awareness of the interrelation of cause and effect, the implications of the general and the particular, the love to sense the figurative in life. These are ways of the mind, and the mind leaves its imprint throughout our word stock.

6

LANGUAGE
TO STRETCH BRAINS WITH

ETYMOLOGY

They were a difficult lot, those linguistic ancestors of ours, but they did us an enduring though gratuitous service. They could be problem neighbors, and they doubtless never meant to promote the welfare of people not their friends, certainly not anybody so remote from them in millennia and continents as we are. Nor were they sophisticated; a proverb about pens being mightier than swords would not have come from them. Yet they bequeathed us a means to stretch our brains.

Understanding their involuntary bequest will take a bit of background. As we have seen in an earlier chapter, we call them Proto-Indo-Europeans (abbreviated PIE; the *Proto-* means early) because their speech accounts for most of the language in Europe and some in Asia as far southeast as India—actually, they were in China, too, but scholars did not know that when the term Indo-European was coined. Beginning about 3000 B.C. they started overrunning their neighbors, moving from their ancient heartland, probably in north-central or eastern Europe, and migrating especially west, south, and southeast. Clearly they were durable and prolific, and may have been uncommonly warlike, although the evidence does not suggest bellicosity. They may simply have been better fitted for aggression; they had tamed horses and had learned to ride them, which may have done it. They had a closely knit authoritarian government, an economy based on agriculture, and permeating religious devotion—assets that helped. Some five thousand years later the languages that have sprung from their dialects dominate all continents except Africa and Asia, and have extensive pockets there.

HOW TO DIG UP YOUR LINGUISTIC ANCESTORS

We must ask how we know about these Indo-Europeans, because we know they could not write. For a few early peoples, mainly the highly civilized ones, we use a method called archaeology, which relies on survival of ancient evidence. Having identified a place where detritus of an early culture may have survived, we excavate, endeavoring to envisage the people and their lives. In this way we know something of the Maya, for example, more about their tools and the work of their hands than about their ideas and the fruit of their brains, but from physical artifacts we can infer some social conduct. Archaeology, however, has narrow limits; some stone crumbles and wood usually rots. Even about the Egyptians we know little before c. 3000 B.C., when they started building their pyramids. Back of that we have stone axes, but who bashed whom with the axes, and why? We do not know.

Another device carries us further back, although usually without providing much detail, because it relies on inference from modern evidence. If we see animals running around on four feet each, and the seashore littered with animals having no feet but with bony coverings, we can make inferences. We will surmise that life lies back of both sorts of creatures, but there must have been changes that differentiated quadrupeds from mollusks. Further examination will tell us more; we can observe that horses are like dogs in having backbones and jointed legs, but differ in that dogs have five claws per foot, horses only one hoof. Now, if we are lucky, if we have enough evidence, particularly if we have a sequence of evidence, we may be able to infer more. With the horse we are lucky because skeletons of many sorts of horses have survived. Thus we know that the horse developed from a small animal about the size of a dog, that it lost two of its toes and became a three-toed horselike creature, and that eventually losing two more toes, it became a one-hoofed horse.

Thus, if we have an assemblage of examples that have evolved, be they dandelions or dolphins, if we have enough different sorts of them and their relatives, we can relate them. We can reconstruct what they must have stemmed from, and we can even establish the lines of development. This was, of course, the approach that permitted Linnaeus to bring order into the botanical kingdom. By studying modern plants, botanists have been able to reconstruct ancestor plants. Later, geologists confirmed such guesses, discovering fossilized plants in rocks.

This same sort of method works in language. The word for horse in Italian is *cavallo,* in Spanish *caballo,* and in French *cheval.* These are enough alike so that anybody would guess they had a common ancestor. If the *o*'s are endings—and endings are common in Italian and Spanish and *o* is one of the most frequent—the words had an ancestor with at least two syllables. The vowels are similar, and we know that minor differences in vowels, especially as reflected in variant spellings, are usual. As for the consonants, the evidence suggests an ancestor with an /l/ at the end of the second syllable (*caval-, cabal-, cheval*). For the first consonant two languages have a *c* in spelling, and /k/ in sound; French is different, having *ch* in spelling and /š/ in sound. But this relationship is everywhere; French *champaigne,* meaning *field,* is Spanish *campo.* English *rich* is French *riche* /rijš/ and Spanish *rico* /rijko/. Accordingly, we would guess that the initial consonant in an ancestor language was /k/ and that /k/ became /š/ as one of the ways French developed. There is another difference; the medial consonant is spelled *v* in Italian and French but *b* in Spanish. We know, however, that a medial sound spelled *b* in Spanish is not much different from /v/ in French and Italian, so that the seeming difference here is more apparent than real. Thus we would guess that *cavallo, caballo,* and *cheval* had an ancestor word something like /kɑvɑl/ plus an ending. Fortunately, we need not guess; we know that the three Romance languages came from Latin, and that in the most widely spoken dialect of Latin the word for horse was *caballo* in the oblique case form, the Latin stop /b/ having become the corresponding fricative /v/. This one example would not be enough to establish the relationships among Italian, Spanish, and French, but when we have thousands of such examples we can reconstruct with confidence, and would not need Latin to prove we are right.

We could go on from these insights. We could notice that the word for men on horseback in English is *cavalry.* We would guess at once that this is our old friend *caballo* in a different dress, and that the word came from Italian or Spanish, or from French before the /k/ changed to /š/. Once more, with enough other evidence, we would be able to generalize as to how Romance words passed into English. That is, if we have plenty of survivals, and particularly if these surviving bits are tolerably durable—bony structures—we can reconstruct with great confidence and to great distances into the past.

Language satisfies one of these conditions beautifully; the evidence of modern language is extensive. But what about durability? Until it was written—and that was late—language lived on the breath, which one might expect to be insubstantial stuff. But not so. Sounds may last for thousands of years with little change, and when they do change they usually shift within narrow limits that can be described linguistically. A /d/ may become its voiceless counterpart /t/; an /e/ may develop a glide and become /ej/ or be lengthened. And these changes are likely to be orderly enough so that the general trend of sound in languages can be charted with remarkable precision. Within limits, even meaning and grammatical use may be durable: *man* has meant a male human primate time out of mind, and the sentences generated by PIE speakers had verbs long before the Egyptians had pyramids.

INDO-EUROPEAN AT HOME AND ABROAD

Now we can return to the Indo-Europeans. During the tens of thousands of years that men have been multiplying and then sweeping over the globe, thousands of dialects and languages have flourished, have moved with migrants and conquerors, obliterating other languages, only to be obliterated in their turn. Modern languages as we know them—as well as so-called dead languages like Classical Greek and Sanskrit—preserve in their spread some evidence of this growth, as clams and horses preserve evidence of anatomic growth.

In both sorts of studies, whether of species or of speech, we can use similar principles; if all quadrupeds have backbones we can assume that the ancestor creature had a backbone, particularly because we can see that a quadruped would need such a connection among its legs. Likewise, if all languages that have descended from PIE have similar words for mothers, we can assume the Proto-Indo-Europeans had a word for mothers, and we can reconstruct it. Even if a few languages have other words for mothers, we can assume that a few were lost—

words are always being lost—and have been replaced. Furthermore, words having limited occurrence also may be revealing; the English word *deep* resembles forms in German, Dutch, and the Scandinavian tongues, all closely related to one another. The word is not found in any other known group of IE languages; accordingly, we would guess that the ancestor of the word *deep* came into languages like English after they had broken off from the ancestors of other IE dialects. Using such methods we can reconstitute a sort of ideal form of the speech we call PIE. We can trace its development from what must have been dialects through intermediate descendant language—which also have been reconstructed—to current bodies of speech like Muscovite Russian.

Incidentally, once we have the language of a people we can know something about the people themselves. The Proto-Indo-Europeans had words for bears and wolves; they apparently feared these creatures, for they had taboos against using the names, probably on the hunt, calling a bear "the brown one," or "the honey-eater." But they had no common words for tigers and lions, even more fearsome predators, nor for hippopotamuses or rhinoceroses. The inference is obvious; speakers of PIE did not live in the tropics. This guess is confirmed by the trees; our words *birch* and *beech* descend from PIE, and as we saw above, the ancestor of *tree* meant also *firm*. On the other hand, PIE contained no word for palm or other tropical foliage. PIE speakers had terms for ice and snow; hence, our linguistic ancestors lived in a temperate climate. Similarly, we know they lived in well-watered country but far from the ocean, because they have words for running water, water standing in pools or lakes, for crossing water, but no words referring to the sea or the food along the seashore. And anything as spectacular and useful as the ocean they could not have failed to notice.

Such evidence suggests that, wherever PIE came from, its speakers lived for a time before their dispersal either in east central Europe or in what is now Russia. The earliest PIE speakers that have been identified with some certainty were living north of the Black and Caspian Seas about 2500 B.C. The fertile plains there may have been the ancestral home of the Proto-Indo-Europeans, but many scholars, noticing the evidence of coldness in the ancient vocabulary, believe it was farther north or northwest. Earlier students believed they had restricted the possible home of PIE more precisely. They noted that the words *beech* and *birch* now refer to trees that had limited spread in Europe. But popular botanical names are notably unstable; the ancestors of *beech* and *birch* as words referred to trees, but to what trees **bhago-* and **bhereg-* referred in PIE nobody knows. The names seem to mean bright or white trees, but such terms would fit the ash as well, perhaps even an oak. (Just to keep the record straight, I will place an asterisk (*) before reconstructed forms. Such shapes are likely to be rather accurate, but idealized, made up from many surviving shapes. Many grammarians use an asterisk to brand ungrammatical expressions. To avoid confusion, I shall not do so in this book.)

As for their culture, the speakers of PIE were not as sophisticated as the Akkads and whoever preceded them in the Tigris-Euphrates valley, or some inhabitants of the great valleys of China, or contemporaries along the Nile and the Ganges. But they were not untutored savages. They had a number of grains, including rye and barley, a simple plow, and some metals—gold, silver, copper, probably bronze, but not as yet iron, for which no common word occurs throughout IE languages. They had learned to tame most common barnyard animals —horses, cattle, pigs, goats, and sheep. They ground grain; they probably wore belted tunics. They had terms for praying and preaching, and for various deities; the name for the Greek god Jupiter comes from **dyeu-pəter,* which can be translated roughly as "God the Father." They had words for faith and law, probably religious law. In short, like some other triumphant invaders—the Mongols in China, for example—they were cultured enough to conquer but less civilized than peoples they overran.

So, some five thousand years ago there began what must be the greatest linguistic movement of all time, the dissemination of the IE languages, and it is not over yet, with Portuguese moving into the upper Amazon valley, Russian overcoming local speech in northern Asia, English expanding in Africa and northern Canada, and the like. IE-speaking peoples moved south in repeated waves; the ancient Hittites in Asia Minor spoke and even wrote an IE dialect. Others traversed southern Asia, leaving speakers of IE in areas now known as Iran and Iraq. Perhaps about 1500 B.C., some speakers of IE broke into the Indian peninsula, bringing with them Sanskrit, the ancestor of a dozen languages and hundreds of dialects, including Hindi, with more than a hundred million speakers. Other IE peoples overran the Balkan Peninsula, leaving behind several languages, including Greek, and this thrust must have been early, because Mycenean Greek was roughly contemporary with Hittite. Somehow speakers of an IE tongue penetrated the Gobi desert when it was less desert than now. IE speakers moved into Russia, or if they were already there, they spread widely, and related languages ringed the Baltic Sea on the south. Some of these Baltic tongues have preserved the PIE inflectional system with only minor changes, and because moving languages are likely to conflict with other languages and change rapidly, conservatism among Baltic speakers suggests they may not have moved far from the IE heartland.

People to whom we attach the name *Italic* moved south and west; those established on the Tiber River have given us Latin, from which have sprung various Romanic tongues, including Italian, French, Spanish, Portuguese, and some others. Peoples we call Celts or Kelts rampaged extensively; they surged south and then spread west and north. What is now France was called Gaul because of them; they were in the Balkan, Italian, and Iberian peninsulas, and even in northern Africa. They overran the British Isles at least twice and survive in the more remote areas, in Ireland, Wales, Scotland, the Isle of Man, Cornwall—the Celtic fringe.

One of the last, and for Americans the most interesting, we call Germanic. Speakers of it moved west and north; in fact, some of those who started east around the Baltic got north into the Scandinavian peninsula, and eventually south and west again. The Franks overran the country beyond the Rhine River, and Gaul became France. Others took over what are now Germany and the Low Countries; some, mostly Angles and Saxons, moved into the British Isles, absorbing the Celts or driving them into the mountains or across the seas into Ireland and Brittany. From the British Isles English spread to North America, Australia, and throughout the world, where for a time the sun never set on the British Empire.

The resulting Germanic speech is one of the most aberrant sorts of IE. In fact, it is so different that some scholars believe Proto-Germanic —the language intermediate between PIE and current Germanic languages—to have been the dialect of some conquered people. However that may be, Germanic speakers were for a time so coherent that modern Germanic languages have common qualities not found elsewhere. For instance, PIE had the consonant /p/, which was preserved in Latin in words like *pater* (father), *pisces* (fish), and *per*, related to various uses of *for*. That is, where Latin has the stop /p/ from PIE, English has the corresponding fricative /f/. And these examples are characteristic; most IE languages not Germanic have a /p/ in such words; Greek has *pater,* Sanskrit has *pitar* for *father.* On the other hand, Germanic languages have a fricative, /f/ or /v/, the German form being *Vater,* Dutch *vader,* Danish and Swedish *fader,* and the like.

Germanic must have existed in at least four subgroups. One would have been South Germanic; it included Burgundian and some other tongues, all vanished with scarcely a trace. Another was East Germanic; it survives as a dead language, unspoken for centuries but preserved in a translation of the Bible. North Germanic survived in Old Norse, from which we have Danish, Swedish, Norwegian, and Icelandic, all called languages although they are not diverse as bodies of speech go —a wit has observed that a language is a dialect with a navy. West Germanic is the best preserved, in two main groups; Old High German is the ancestor of Modern German, and along the sea Low Germanic has sired Dutch, Walloon, Frisian, and English, the latter usually divided into Old English (preserved in works dated c. 700 or a little earlier to about 1100), Middle English (1100–1500 or a little earlier), and Modern English to date, the latter dialects called Current English or Present-Day English.

VOCABULARY AND THE COMMON TOUCH

We are told that God created order out of a void, but if so, such creation is a property of deity. Some of what man does with language is godlike, but not on the whole his word formation. Mostly, when he creates words he has to start with something and reform it.

Of what early man used we remain vastly ignorant, although some terms must have come from imitating sounds. Algonkin Canadian Indians call an owl an *u-hoo* for obvious reasons, and words like *papa* and *mama* reflect the babbling of infants, but most words in known languages must have come from linguistic materials long in existence. In the previous chapter we noticed that many words have been reformed into their current named uses, even relatively recently, but they *are* re-formed. Lewis Carroll coined a few shapes as part of a joke, but for all the attention attracted by Jabberwocky, *wabe* and *gimble* have not become words, and *mime,* which already existed as a shape, has not imported other senses from beyond the Looking Glass.

Pretty obviously, the materials with which minds work when they develop new named uses are of two sorts: modern man gets meanings out of himself and his life, but he acquires linguistic shapes—sounds, printed words, or whatever—mainly from other languages or earlier languages. Again, these last are of two sorts; some descend from an ancestor language, of which the oldest we know in the English-speaking tradition is PIE; others are borrowed, however changed, from foreign languages, as we have recently borrowed *sputnik* and *pizza*. First we might notice that each body of words that makers of English have used for shapes, and in part for meanings, has its characteristic qualities. Below a few are compared. To the left are native words that have descended from Old English; to the right are words of similar meaning borrowed into English since OE times:

OE	*Borrowed*
about	approximately
cow	bovine
dead	necrosed
house	edifice
man	*Homo sapiens*
run	function
to	proceeding (toward)
yes	certainly

The native words are shorter, better known, and involved in more uses.

Admittedly, I have stacked the evidence a bit. I could have found a few short, common, borrowed words with many uses, like *camp* and *faith,* but they would be relatively few and would include none of the smallest and most used words like *the, of, and, to, a, in, that, is, was, he, for,* and *it,* the dozen commonest words in the language. In fact, even in edited English, words like *the* and *of* occur forty or fifty times as frequently as the commonest words borrowed from the Latin tradition, words like *just, state,* and *people,* and in spoken English the popularity of native words would be even greater.

On the other hand, no long words derive from English except compounds like *firearm* and *householder,* and few rare words survive except obsolete terms or uses. Old English *cop* did not mean a policeman but did mean the top of a hill, a board to mark a beehive, or a measure of peas. As for borrowed words, a random sampling would include *chemiluminescence* and *pseudepigraphical.* If one were to list all words borrowed into English the child who knows most of the native words would be likely to recognize only 1 or 2 percent of the borrowed words, and even a highly educated adult would never have heard of half of them. Likewise, almost all native words have many uses and most borrowed words have few; for all the native words in the list above I could have found a dozen uses, most of them without borrowed one-word synonyms. *Get* has at least fifty uses and appears in scores of phrases, but many borrowed words have only one use. In short, a large random sampling would only confirm the conclusions obvious in the selected examples above.

Any results as spectacular as the difference between native and borrowed words in English must have causes. They do, and some causes appear readily from the history of Old and Middle English. We have seen that Old English stems from peoples who had been living on or near the North Sea in northern Europe; the immigrants included two rather numerous groups, the Angles and the Saxons, along with some people called the Jutes, whoever they were. They brought with them assorted Germanic dialects, and we have seen earlier that Proto-Germanic was on the move and in conflict with Celtic. We have noticed changes in pronunciation; there were changes, also, in grammar, with inflections simplifying and even disappearing, so that many native English words have lost everything but the syllable embodying the root idea, and even part of that. Our word *say,* two phonemes /sej/, can appear in such forms as *gesaegde, secgende, and gesecganne.* On the other hand, although many borrowed words contain a simple root, this syllable had already been built up before it was borrowed; *predicament* contains a root syllable *-dic-* implying *say,* seen in words like *diction,* but other bits had been added to it before it was borrowed.

So much for early English linguistic shapes. But society also influenced word choice. Beginning in 1066, much of England was overrun by the Norman French; French became the official language. Learning and the professions—including much of the law—were directed through the church, which used Latin. English was spoken by the uneducated, by the poor, by laborers (mostly farm laborers) and somewhat in the homes of people who knew French or Latin. It was thus a humble if useful tongue; it was used for work, for everyday living. Words like *life* and *death, eat* and *sleep* are native; they persisted because even common people needed them. Farmers and housewives outnumbered courtiers and nuns; people spent more time working (from OE *weorc*) than they did adjudicating (from Latin *adjudicare*). Hence English triumphed over French and Latin, and the common terms preserved the words ordinary folk used in their homey doings; the borrowed words are generally more esoteric, terms associated with less usual activity. And because the native words were common terms, they have grown the fastest; on the whole, in language, the more uses a word has, the more new uses it is likely to acquire. It is the linguistic equivalent of "to him who hath shall be given."

7

LANGUAGE
TO STRETCH BRAINS WITH

APPLICATION

We may now be able to make use of all this. We have seen that of linguistic shapes used to suggest meaning in English we have two sorts, each with characteristic qualities and uses. Native words have mainly come from PIE, although some few had been borrowed from other sources, from non-Germanic neighbors of the Angles and Saxons, and the like. They were the handy, practical terms that the relatively unsophisticated Germanic invaders lived with. They had been still further simplified and still further reduced to a sort of basic vocabulary during the centuries when English served mainly for the daily living of ordinary folk. Old English included most of the words that every child would know and everybody used, the words for familiar objects (*bread, road*) and the grammatical words (*the, he, that, of, in*). Nobody had to learn such words consciously; they were so instinctive in the life of any cottage that children grew up with them almost as naturally as they learned to crawl.

Borrowed words were different. They were harder to learn, and most people who know them at all have had to learn many of them deliberately. They tend to be long words; native words tend to be one syllable (*walk*) or a compound of familiar syllables (*sidewalk*). Affixes used to build up such words are few and well-known; anybody who knows *walk* will know at once what *walked* and *walking* are good for. But borrowed words tend to be long, as we have seen, and they may be made of strange elements. Not everybody who knows what a graph is could figure out what *pseudepigraphical* means. Thus almost all the hard words, those that have to be consciously learned, are borrowed.

And here cognates come in. The word derives from *co-gnatus*, compounded of *co-* meaning *with* and *gnatus*, related to our word *genus*, meaning born. That is, cognates are words born together, which is another way of saying they had the same ancestor. For English, since it is an IE language, most of the ancestors were something in PIE. For example, the English word *saw*, something to cut with, goes back to the PIE root **sek-*, meaning to cut. The same root came down into Latin, from which we get *segment* and *section*, the results of things being cut up. That is, English *saw* and Latin *secare*, from which we get words like *section* and *dissect*, are cognates; they were "born together" in PIE **sek-*.

At this point we might make a practical observation; this fact of there being cognates can be used to help speakers of English learn vocabulary. Most words borrowed into English have descended through another language. This need not have been so. Borrowing comes by association; Japanese has borrowed many terms from Chinese, a language not closely related, because China was the nearby power. American English has borrowed some words from Algonkin Indian, words like *woodchuck* and *quahog*, because the Indians were here first. But the great bulk of English borrowing involves other IE languages, Latin and French most of all, but Greek, Italian, Spanish, Danish-Norwegian, Dutch, German, and others. Thus for any rare or difficult word borrowed into English, there is likely to be at least one native cognate everybody knows, a term in the native word stock. If you have trouble learning, or learning to use, words like *dissection, intersect, segmental*, or even *saxifrage*, the whole job becomes simpler if you start with the English cognate *saw* and relate the borrowed words to it. But who would guess, without some key, that when the surgeon uses a *saw* to *dissect* he is using two forms of the same word through cognates that go back to **sek-*, to cut?

SOUND CHANGE AND THE INDO-EUROPEAN BRAIN-STRETCHER

Changes in sound provide the key, in fact, a whole key ring of keys. We have already seen one of these unlocking a mystery. Latin *pater* pretty much preserves the PIE word for a male parent, which became *father* in English and something beginning with /f/ or /v/ in the other Germanic tongues. We noticed others; Latin *pisces* equated with English *fish,* and Latin *por* or *per* with English *for.* We could have added hundreds more—*plate* from Latin as against English *flat, five* from OE as against *pentagon* from Latin. In fact, there are so many that we could enunciate a principle, that a /p/ in PIE may be expected to survive in Latin and in most other PIE languages, but in native English words the stop is likely to become a corresponding fricative, voiceless /f/ or voiced /v/.

Now let us look at the second consonant in Latin *pater* and English *father.* Here a /t/, another voiceless stop in PIE, has become a voiced fricative /ð/. Again, we could find hundreds of examples of this change; in Latin *mater* as against English *mother, tavern* from Latin as against *thorp,* which appears in English place-names. Is it then true that all voiceless stops in PIE remained unchanged in Latin but became fricatives in English? There is supporting evidence. PIE had a root **kerd-.* The initial consonant appears as /k/ in Latin—although spelled *c*—which was borrowed into English in such words as *cornet,* a little horn, and *cardiac,* referring to the heart. The corresponding words that descended into English are *horn* and *heart.* Here the initial sound in OE is one mentioned in Chapter 2—/χ/, the fricative corresponding to /k/. Thus, the voiceless stop in PIE has become the corresponding fricative in English, and then has lost enough of its friction to become the aspirate /h/. There are hundreds of examples. A variant of the sound was preserved in Latin and borrowed into English in such words as *quote, quotient.* The same sound descended into English as a fricative and then the aspirate, giving us such words as *who, what,* and *which.* Thus the words *what quality* are cognates going back to an old relative and interrogative, the native word with /h/ the borrowed word with /kw/, represented in the French spelling *qu.*

We might try a similar approach with the IE voiced stops. Look at the following sequence: *dual, two; dental, tooth; dictate, teach; decimal, ten.* Again the same sort of thing has happened, although the details are different. In the list of words the first is borrowed from Latin, the second descends directly into English. That is, a voiced stop /d/ is preserved in Latin but becomes the corresponding voiceless stop /t/ in English. As usual, there are numerous examples. Similarly, PIE had a voiced bilabial stop /b/, which appears in words like *bucket* and *buckboard* borrowed through Latin, and with the voiceless bilabial stop /p/ in English words such as *pouch* and *pocket.*

This could be carried on and on through all the consonants and many languages, although not all of them show as much variety as do plosives going into English. In fact the patterns of drift have been elaborated in a statement called Grimm's Law (for one of the brothers Grimm, professors who collected Grimm's fairy tales), describing movements that unite and distinguish the various bodies of speech in the great IE language family. IE consonants fall into patterns because when they changed they usually drifted in an orderly way, in ways that can be described linguistically; voiced sounds became voiceless or vice versa, stops became fricatives or fricatives sharpened into stops, aspiration was increased or declined.

All this gets too complicated to be traced here, and most of it does not help much in learning English vocabulary. What does help is the movement described above, often called the Germanic Sound Shift, that occurred before Proto-Germanic broke away from other IE languages—the shift that, as we have seen, makes us say *fish* but pronounce borrowed words about fishing *piscatorial* and *piscivorous,* with /p/ and /sk/. This movement had shifts within it—Verner's Law, for example, accounts for such differences as /ð/ in English where /t/ appears in German, in *father* and *mother* as against *Vater* and *Mutter,* but that is a complication we can do without.

One other observation must be made about consonants. We noticed above that our *saw* is related to Latin words having the syllable *-sect-*. A rhyming word, *law* resembles *saw* in that it is related to words having somewhat similar consonants: *ledger, lochia, log, stalag.* Related to *lay,* they all have something to do with lying down or having been set down—a *log* is "the lying-down one." The root is **legh-* or **leg-*, and phonetically one can readily see what has happened. From the English form the consonant has disappeared, but in various languages this consonant has taken odd quirks, being preserved as /g/ or becoming /č/ or /ǰ/. Now, we should notice that the symbol *gh* is an attempt to suggest a back palatal consonant. Palatals do not behave as do most other consonants. A /p/ or a /b/ is firmly fixed; made by the lips, it stays at the lips. But palatals are made by the tongue against the roof of the mouth, and they change with the point at which the tongue contacts the structures above it. And as the tongue moves to make vowels, a palatal consonant, if it is adjacent to a vowel, will move with it.

To see how this shift works, pronounce a sequence like *meek hawk* slowly and carefully. You will see that the consonant /k/ moves forward after the front vowel in *meek* and back after the back vowel in *hawk*. Accordingly, palatals are unstable sounds; almost anything can happen when adjacent vowels move or when accents shift. Modern English *law* comes from OE *lagu*. That is, /lɔgu/ has become /lɔ/; the palatal has vanished and a vowel with it. This sort of thing happened commonly. Consider the English word *laugh*. In OE it was pronounced something like /χlijəχɑn/. The palatals are gone, and one of them has been replaced by a voiceless fricative /f/. Something similar occurred when OE *enoh* /enɔχ/ became Modern English *enough* /ənʌf/. Perhaps for the moment all we need say is that palatals are unstable by nature, and any of a number of changes can be expected to appear through them.

Thus far, we have considered consonants. But vowels can show variety too, including one pervasive early quirk, and another later drift. The first stems from PIE itself, which made use of what is sometimes call *ablaut* (in German meaning change of sound), change of an internal vowel. Some of these patterns have survived in English sequences like *sing, sang, sung; write, wrote, written.* Many more permeated PIE dialects; descended into various languages, they have altered millions of words. Consider *tooth* and its relatives, mentioned above. The root was **dent-*, which in its full form in Latin was borrowed into English *dental, dentistry,* along with *indentation,* which might be freely translated "putting a tooth into something," and even *indenture,* a document raggedly torn as though it has tooth marks. This **dent-* came into Proto-Germanic with what is called 0-grade—in other words it has /o/ rather than /e/ as vowel—which gives us English *tooth.* Meanwhile, a different variant of the 0-grade went into Greek, where it came out as a syllable *-dont-,* seen in words like *orthodontist,* meaning one who straightens teeth, *ortho-* being related to our word *order.*

The later movement, often called the Great English Vowel Shift, was restricted to English, centering in the fifteenth and sixteenth centuries, although it continued later in many dialects. In this shift certain vowels, mainly the tenser and longer vowels, developed glides and moved, mainly forward and upward. This, again, is an orderly, describable progression. Vowels move rather readily because they are not tied to fixed points like the lips and teeth; they can be elongated and can break into diphthongs. For *get,* of which the standard pronunciation is /get/, southeastern American dialects may have /gijət/, a diphthong. Conversely, a diphthong can be simplified; *law,* which as we have seen was once /lɑgu/ or /lɔgu/ became something like /lɔwə/ as the palatal consonant lost some of its fricative quality, then /lɔə/, and now it can be pronounced with a relatively pure vowel /lɔ/.

All this gets a bit complicated, but as a rule of thumb we can make the following statements about English vowels as they appear as words or syllables in native words or words borrowed early:

Slack vowels will not change much; OE *hil* is Mod. E. *hill,* both pronounced /hil/.

Most vowels in stressed syllables developed glides and moved forward; *me* in OE /mej/ or /me:/ (two dots can be used to indicate a long, pure vowel) became Mod. E. /mij/.

A few stressed vowels and diphthongs did not move forward, even moved back or toward the center of the mouth; OE *hus* /hus/ became Mod. E. *house* (hɑʊs/; OE *rid* /rijd/ became Mod. E. *ride* /raid/.

Vowels in unaccented syllables tend to become schwa or /i/ or to fall out completely; as was noticed above, *the* can be /ðij/, /ði/, /ðə/, or even /ð/, especially before a vowel as in "the only one" /ðounli wən/.

These changes, except the last, did not usually affect words borrowed after the time of the vowel shift; *maintain,* borrowed late, would presumably now be pronounced like "mean teen" if it had been borrowed early enough.

Just to bring details together, a summary of the consonant changes that most extensively involve English may be handy, and for ready reference I shall use spelling:

ch in English may equate with *k, g, c* (often pronounced /č/ as in *choose*). Many spellings *ch* or *sh* stem from changes in English or French; the result is the same, although the drifts were later than PIE.

f may equate with *p,* as in *father, pater.*

gh may be preserved in spelling where a palatal has ceased to be pronounced or has become a vowel.

h may equate with *k, g, c* (often pronounced /s/ if the word has come through French), as in *heart* as against *cordial, hundred* as against *century.*

p may equate with *b,* as in *pouch* as against *bucket.*

t may equate with *d* as in *tooth* as against *dentist.*

th may equate with *d* or *t,* as in *father, pater; three, trio.*

wh may equate with *qu,* as in *who, quality.*

w, a rounded semivowel, may equate with *v;* it may appear without apparent warning and disappear without a trace, as in *work, organ; weave, verse.*

r may seem to move to the other side of a vowel; Chaucer calls a bird a *brid.*

Then there is a sort of blanket explanation. "Catch 22" in Robert Heller's novel by that title takes care of everything for which there is no other specific catch—that is, there will always be a catch to everything. The etymological equivalent might be called "Etymological Quirk 22—there will always be another quirk you don't know about." The fact is that only the broad outlines of etymology are simple; in practice the whole becomes complex, with minor movements, rare drifts, seeming exceptions, and principles getting in one another's way. Perhaps the best solution is to enunciate Quirk 23, which might read, "Okay, so what?" Or, in other words, minor lapses and seeming inconsistencies can best be ignored by anybody but the specialists. For practical purposes one can usually trust the etymologists, particularly if one relies only on good ones.*

---

* Perhaps comment is in order. For advanced work—although not for all research—the best book generally available is *The American Heritage Dictionary* because of the excellent list of PIE roots and cognates in the appendix, but many beginners find it too difficult to use. For clarity, accuracy, and succinctness, most users will find *Webster's New World Dictionary,* second edition, the handiest. Two superb books

THE BRAIN-STRETCHER IN ACTION

We are now ready to observe the brain-stretcher at work. Biologically, brains are neither growable nor renewable. Brain cells can take over new functions, and thus damaged brains can repair themselves in the sense that they can find other ways of doing their job, but apparently not by growing new brain parts. Neither exercise nor vitamins will do that. But most of us who would welcome better brains do not need to grow bigger ones or new brain cells. Nobody, as far as we know, has ever used all the brains he has as well as he might. Thus anyone wanting more brain power has only to use better the brains he already has, and to stretch brains language provides a useful tool. As we have seen, language is a multifarious thing, but notably having more brain power is having more vocabulary. Again, vocabulary is not one thing; the Anglo-Saxons had a revealing word for it, calling it a word-hoard. They seem to have understood that the more words one has, the more living and thinking and feeling he has been able to invest in words, the richer he is, at least intellectually. Accordingly, let us see how the IE brain-stretcher can grow vocabulary.

Assume you have encountered the word *ergonomics* and you do not know what it means and fear you will find it hard to remember. The first step, of course, is to consult a good dictionary, where you will find that the word means the study of relationships among workers and working in society. Some of all this is suggested by the similarity of *ergonomics* to *economics,* but what about the *erg-*? If you will now look up the etymology you will find that the root is **werg-*, meaning to do something, seen in our word *work*. Thus the Greek word *erg* means a unit of work, and *ergonomics* is the economics of work. The shapes of *erg* and *work* are superficially different, but using what you now know about the ways sound descended into various Indo-European languages you can explain all this. As we have seen (in the list of conso-

provide more detail: *The Oxford Dictionary of English Etymology* and *Klein's Comprehensive Etymological Dictionary of the English Language. Origins: A Short Etymological Dictionary of Modern English* is older and less reliable, but is generally sound and for most users may be the most engaging of all. Unfortunately, some excellent dictionaries, including the *Oxford* and various editions of the *New International* contain few IE roots.

nant changes, p. 87), *w* represents a rounding of simple breath, and can readily disappear before a vowel. We have noticed that /g/ is only the voiced form of /k/ (*ch*, p. 87), and we know that many consonants voiced in PIE remained voiced in most IE languages but became voiceless in English. So, that is it; *erg* and *work* mean much the same and are orderly developments by two different lines of descent from PIE. Non-specialists had probably best take most differences in vowels on faith (Quirk 23), although there is usually an explanation, and there is one here. In many dialects of Old English the word was *werc,* and our spelling with an *o* comes from another dialect.

So now you have the key to guessing words you have never seen before. You will know what an *ergograph* and an *ergometer* are, because you probably know, or can readily find out, what *graph* and *meter* mean. You will probably surmise, or you can readily discover that **werg-* came through Latin with 0-grade, so that *organ* is something that makes music, and *organization* is something that works, and that when somebody *organizes* the *workers* they are only working the workers into something that works. You probably know words like *energy, allergy, liturgy,* and *dramaturgy,* but even if you do you are likely to have more feeling for them once you see in them the syllable *-erg-* that means *work,* and you will know better how to use them yourself and to interpret them when others use them. That is, knowing that *-erg-* is the word *work* in a different form will permit you to learn a dozen or a score of words more readily and remember them better than you could have, had you learned *ergograph* by itself. You can stretch your brain with a little IE leverage.

But we are not quite done with *work* and its relatives. The root came into English in a suffixed, 0-grade shape, the **werg-* being reduced to something like *wrk*. It then picked up a suffix having a /t/ in it. Thus the word in OE was often spelled *wyrhta,* pronounced /wijrχtə/. Later the ending fell off, the palatal was no longer pronounced (*gh,* p. 87), and (ex. 2, p. 86) in accordance with the English Vowel Shift /ij/ became /ai/. The result is our word *wright,* a workman, especially a skilled workman. A *wheelwright* was the special carpenter who made wheels; an ancestor of Mr. *Cartwright* must have made carts. If you had not known before you now know why a *playwright* is named as he is; he makes plays, and you can guess why the word is commonly misspelled either *playwrite* or *playright,* on the false etymologies that he is the person who writes plays or has the right to them.

To suggest that utilities observable in *work* and its relatives are not unique, let us try another. We might start with any of hundreds of words beginning with *p*, such as *parvenu, paramount, portend, perfect, prefabrication,* and *proton*. We could find that they all go back to **per-*, which had already developed various uses as prepositions and verbs even in PIE. Knowing (*f*, p. 87) that a /p/ in the mother language became /f/ in Germanic descendants, we need not be surprised that **per-* became English *for;* if you are *for* somebody you are a *pro*ponent. The PIE speakers whom we have been discussing were our *fore*fathers, who spoke the *par*ent tongue. In OE, as we have seen, a word *faran* developed, meaning to go *for*ward, so that a *for*d was a place to go across water and a *fer*ry a means of being taken over. You may *fare* well with wel*fare*. There were combinations like *for*give and *fore*warn, because *for-* became a *pre*fix in English as *per-* and *pro-* did in Latin and Greek. The im*port* of the im*por*tation of **per-* from these languages was *pro*found and *per*vading, and it goes on *per*petually, a *pre*cious heritage, *pri*mary for vocabulary. The knowledge that *for* is only a *par*allel *pro*nunciation can *pro*mote com*pre*hension, and the *pro*pinquity of cognates can discourage *for*getting.

8

LANGUAGE
TO WORK WITH

BORROWING, AFFIXING

Minds, we have seen, culture words and other wordlike counters of meaning. Words grow as they do because human minds work the way they do. But why should language grow at all? Why does it not vegetate once it is extensive enough so that people can communicate with it? Why does it not die, as plants and animals do?

Many languages have, of course. Hundreds of languages were formerly spoken in what is now the United States. Most of these native tongues are silenced, their earthly remains entombed in scholarly monographs. Navaho survives, protected by the reaches of semidesert; some Eskimo speech continues precariously, protected by a frigid climate. But all native speech in the Americas is apparently moribund, and death seems to be the fate of most languages everywhere; they die because their speakers are killed—smallpox and firewater were among the great destroyers of American Indian languages—or because the offspring of native speakers learn a different language. English replaces Delaware; Spanish supersedes Nahuatl. Some languages, relatively few, survive through their descendants so that, as we have seen, PIE lives today on all continents through such current speech as Hindi, Polish, and Australian English. That is, all languages as individual bodies of language are doomed, as mortal as men or butterflies, but languages seem always either to grow or die, and some few grow so mightily and so long that they promise through reproduction to live forever.

So we might ask why language grows. But first we should look at some growing language, and we may as well choose English, partly because it has special interest for readers who are likely to pick up this book, and partly because few languages, if any, have grown so fast and spread so far so rapidly.

GROWTH OF THE ENGLISH WORD-HOARD

We have already encountered English in its earliest known form, PIE. It was the speech of an obscure tribal group, relatively remote from the best culture of the day. (The Sumers, to the south, were already writing.) A small body of simple folk, their language was adequate for its users, but the needs of those users were modest. PIE served for farmers who tended animals, grew a few grains, and observed the rural world around them, especially to hunt and fish successfully. These earliest Indo-Europeans could travel, but until their great migrations started, did not very much. They had families, and they could communicate within the family; they had some social relationships, mostly the extension of the family into a simple government. They practiced a vigorous but primitive sort of religion, with deities closely associated to the world and its wonders. Many subjects never came up; air did not need to be tested for pollution. In fact we have no evidence that these rather factual-minded people knew that there is any such thing as air. They breathed, but even their word for breathing seems to have been related to boiling (our word *brew*) as evidenced in steam. They knew about wind; they could feel wind even though they could not see air, and our words like *air* and *ventilate* come from *we-*, to blow. The Proto-Indo-Europeans had the words they needed, but we have no evidence of more than a few thousand terms, and these were embodied in roots expressive of the commonest ideas—getting food and eating it, getting children and rearing them—but few social problems and little philosophy.

When the Proto-Germanic peoples moved north they encountered the sea. Understandably this revelation moved all through their language. For many of the new words of Germanic origin an etymological dictionary can only say "origin unknown," "not attested in Indo-

European," "possibly related to ————," and the like. Almost all Germanic languages that have survived have words for the sea, which must have come from a term something like *saiwiz*, but where did *saiwiz* come from? Not from the PIE we know. It may have been made up from some PIE root that has not survived; more likely, it was borrowed from the speech of peoples who lived along the shore—whom the Proto-Germanic peoples overran—from one of those thousands of languages that did not survive, possibly from some relative of Basque, known otherwise only in the Pyrenees Mountains. *Sail* and *to sail* are similarly "unattested." So is *ship*, although most Germanic languages have it. A few words were adapted from PIE; *whale* and *walrus* mean merely "big fish"—the Proto-Germans did not know that whales are mammals. For them, whales were only the big fish to end all big fishes; seemingly whales were so big that a word like Old English *hwael* or Old High German *walira* was no longer suitable for any other big fish.

LOAN WORDS COME TO OUR LINGUISTIC ANCESTORS

The Angles, Saxons, and Jutes were living along the North Sea in the early centuries of the Christian era when something new began to happen to them and to affect their language. They encountered Roman traders occasionally, even had to fight Roman soldiers, by Germanic standards men unbelievably well-equipped. They did not know, these unsophisticated forest- and seaside-dwellers, that they were witnessing a local, minor manifestation of the growth of the mighty Roman Empire that was to change the map of the Mediterranean world. What they knew was that they could now buy better pots and pans than they could before, better and cheaper—*pan* seems to be a borrowed word, perhaps the same as Latin *patina*.

Then, in several waves, mostly before 500 A.D., groups of these Germanic speakers moved to the neighboring island of Britain, partly because the Romans who had already conquered the island went home. They overran the Celts, and once they had settled down they kept getting more culture from the south, even the Christian religion. Again, what they did not know was that a great new movement had begun: for hundreds of years the dominant fact of English history was to be that Mediterranean culture would flow north toward them, bringing

new tools, new arts and professions, new techniques, new ways of thinking and working, even such esoterica as writing and written works.
They did not know, either, that something must be done linguistically
to adjust to all this new living. They did not need to know; language
always takes care of such needs, and English rose to the occasion.

In part the Anglo-Saxons just used old words in new ways, as we
have seen earlier that man does naturally. Consider *love*. The word
seems to have meant something like *like, trust, have faith;* other grades
of the term give us such words as *belief, leave* (a noun meaning permis-
sion), *libido*. Soon, with a new and more philosophic religion, the old
word *love* came to encompass God's love, the love of God, and love as
an idea or principle. The Anglo-Saxons also combined old words in
new ways; what we call the Bible (from oriental *Biblos*), they called
Godspell (God's story), our word *gospel*. *Goldhoard* became a word
for the treasury—doubtless the older Indo-Europeans had kept most
of their wealth on the hoof; they had gold, but not enough of it to
have a gold standard.

Some vocabulary came in by the simple process of adopting a new
word along with the new thing. Thus a harbor improved to accom-
modate the great Roman ships became a *port* (Latin *portus*); the fine
roads built by the Romans were called *streets* (Latin *strada*), which
were measured in *miles* (*mille passum,* a thousand paces), along which
came a wonderful new intoxicating drink, *wine* (Latin *vinum*). Especially there were words associated with the new religion, our terms
apostle, deacon, demon, devil, hymn, pope, priest, school, and the like.
Meanwhile, for some centuries life did not change greatly in the British
Isles, and there was no great flood of new words. A few terms were
picked up from the native Celts, mostly place-names, as was noted in
Chapter 2.

Some terms came in through conquests. Beginning in the ninth century, Danes and Norwegians overran parts of the island. They spoke
North Germanic dialects, by now rather different from the West Germanic speech that included Old English. Many of the invaders, somewhat subdued, stayed on in the north and east in what was called
Danelaw, and some of their speech became localized. Proto-Germanic
had a sound /sk/; it survived in Old Norse but had changed in Old
English to /š/, often spelled *sh*. Thus, Mod. E. (Modern English) may
have doublets, one from Scandinavian speakers spelled *sk,* one from
Old English spelled *sh*. There was an old Germanic term **skurt,* mean-

ing short, used for "the short one," an undergarment worn under mail. This had been changed in Old English to give our word *shirt;* the same word had been little changed in Old Norse, and has survived in our word *skirt. Skill* from Old Norse has the same root as *shield* and *shell.* Similarly, Old Norse *sistyr* replaced the OE *sweoster,* two forms of the same word. Old Norse third-person plural pronouns replaced the Old English forms, so that we now use *they, their, them* rather than the OE *hie, hierra, hiem.*

More change resulted from a later invasion. These folk, too, had come from Scandinavia, but they had sojourned in France, acquired a French dialect, and were called Normans—that is, men from the north. In 1066 they conquered most of the area now known as England, killed many of the more powerful and educated natives, and set themselves up as rulers. Inevitably, they took over the government, the church, the school system insofar as there was one, the more important business and professional posts, and the like. Norman French became the official language, and words referring to governmental activities appeared in the local French dialect, known as Anglo-Norman. A legislative body became a *parlement* (which in French means only *a talking*); minor officers of various sorts became *serjeants,* the word a doublet with *servant;* a royal residence or a seat of justice became a *court,* from a Latin word meaning an enclosure—the same term from PIE, **gher-,* has given us also *garden, guard, warden* and the like. Beasts were still tended by Anglo-Saxon menials as *cows, calves, swine,* and *sheep,* but when the meat was prepared by an Anglo-Norman *butcher (bouchere)* and served at the *table* of an Anglo-Norman baron or duke (the Anglo-Saxons ate at a *board*), it became Anglo-Norman *beef, veal, pork,* and *mutton.* (Incidentally, Walter Scott is usually given credit for this observation, but he apparently picked it up from the lexicographer Bailey.)

A DELUGE OF DICTION

Thus for a time there were few broad changes in either English life or English vocabulary. Then the flood started. By 1200 England was part of a great Norman empire stretching from Scotland to Sicily, with strong connections to Africa and the Arabic east. New goods flowed north, even luxuries like spices—gentlemen and fine ladies no longer had to eat rotten meat—and new sciences appeared, alchemy and astrology. New words poured in so fast that during the first half of the thirteenth century English acquired more new terms than had been recorded since the coming of the Germanic invaders. The flood continued, and in the second half of the century, more terms were borrowed than had been recorded previously, including the first half of the century. And in the fourteenth century, again, more words came than in all previous known time, and the pace set by 1350 continued for centuries and then declined slowly.

We might look at samples. Here is a sentence from the Peterborough version of the Old English Chronicle for the year 1137:

> Þa þe king Stephene to Englalande com, þa macod he his gadering aet Oxenford, and þar nam þe biscop Roger of Seriberi, Alexander biscop of Lincoln, hise neues, and did aelle in prisun til he iafen up here castles.

The passage means that when King Stephen came to England and had convened an assembly at Oxford, he seized two bishops, his nephews, and put them in prison until they surrendered their castles. Neither the event nor the language was as unusual as one might expect. Stephen had the inhospitable practice of suspending selected guests by their thumbs, and as for the language, the author was a learned man, doubtless a trilinguist fluent in French and Latin as well as English, but he uses mainly native English except for official terms. *Biscop* was a title, and *castles* and *prisons* were Norman institutions. All the other words but one are native, *neues* (nephews), which was handier than Old English *sister's son* or *brother's son.* The castles were not surrendered; they were *iafen up* (given up). Even the official conference was not *assembled;* the king made (*macod*) his *gathering.*

Now let us drop down a century and a half; Chaucer's poor Parson is speaking:

> Also verray shrifte axeth certeine condiciouns. First, that thow shryve thee by thy free will, noght constreyned, ne for shame of folk, ne for maladie, ne swiche thinges. For it is resoun that he that trespaseth by his free wyl, that by his fre wyl he confesse his trespas.

Here we might note that the author has not changed much, but the language has. In education and way of life, Chaucer's Parson would not have differed essentially from the Peterborough monk, but he uses many more borrowed words, mostly from Latin through French: *verry* (meaning *true*), *certein* (now spelled *certain*), *condiciouns* (*conditions*), *constreyned* (*constrained*), *maladie* (*sickness* was available, although not yet *illness*), *resoun* (*reason*), *trespaseth* and *trespas* (*sin* was available for either the noun or the verb), and *confesse.* Here the words involved in grammar continue to be native, as they had been for centuries, but now more than half the names were borrowed. And that practice continued, until in Modern English all prose is seeded with borrowed words, terms so much acclimated that only the learned know which are native and which are not.

Notably, these words responded to a demand. Chaucer's Parson is using the terminology of theological discussion; there were few such words in Old English. Legendary heroes like Hengist and Horsa did not need to deliberate about salvation; they could settle disputes by butchering the disputants. But their descendants had to discuss more and slaughter less; even the militants needed good armor, and the best came from the Continent, bringing French words with it. The new law brought French and Latin terms like *tort, misdemeanor,* and *testatrix.* The new learning brought *doctors,* even *surgeons.* The new music brought French *ballades,* and eventually Italian *concerti.* In almost everything there were new activities, bringing a tide of new words.

Thus, a language always responds to fill the needs of its users, but now the whole pattern of English acquisition of vocabulary changed. Borrowing there had always been, of course, but on the whole when Anglo-Saxons needed new words they developed a compound from within the language. But beginning in the thirteenth century, Englishmen opted for foreign words. Probably the borrowing was made easier because, for centuries, educated Englishmen were bilingual or trilingual, and most of the borrowed words came from Latin or French, or from Greek through these languages. Perhaps the foreign words came in such a flood that the local phrase-makers were inundated. But whatever reason the linguistic habits of speakers of English shifted.

Of course compounding did not cease; for new inventions—especially if these did not come from abroad—new terms could be devised. New means of travel could be called *steamboats, steamships, railroads,* and *railways*—though *rail* is a borrowed word—and such native compounds were mingled with borrowings like *locomotive* and *transportation systems.* In fact, as we shall see below, American English was to reverse the process again, but for centuries after about 1200 borrowing was so

lively that the great bulk of entries in any dictionary of English will
be loan words or terms put together out of borrowed elements, many
of them brought in during this period.

TO BORROW IS TO REINVENT

But importing has side effects, and the terms *loan word* and *borrow-ing* may mislead us. If I borrow my neighbor's only ladder, he has no
ladder until I take it back, but if we borrow the word *pizza,* Italian
speech is no poorer even though we never return it. Futhermore, if I
borrow a ladder, the object I have is the same one my neighbor had,
and barring mistreatment, it will be the same object when I return it.
But a loan word is not like a ladder, and borrowing in a linguistic
sense is not like borrowing in a neighborly sense. The locution I borrow
is never the same as the term in the original language. So much is
involved in the simplest word, so much of local pronunciation, of con-
voluted meaning, of social climate, that moving any one linguistic bit
from one language and culture into another without change is impossible. In language, to borrow is to alter the borrowed object.

Change by borrowing appears readily in pronunciation. The American beer, *High Life,* is called /ijlijf/ in French, as though it were
spelled *ee-leef,* because a literate Frenchman, looking at the spelling
high life would be likely to pronounce it as though it is French. For
the same reason, in Mexico the beer is called /ijglifej/, as though it
were spelled *eeg-ly-fay.* Even a Mexican who knows English, unless he
is fluent in the language, would not be able to say /hailaif/ with an
American accent, and if he could he would be but one in so many tens
of thousands that he would have little impact on Mexican Spanish.
Lately, the Chinese have been importing Yorkshire boars to improve
the strain of Chinese pigs; the beasts are called something like *Yok-a-
shah.*

Change in meaning will be less obvious but probably more permeating. Consider PIE **kamp-,* which meant to bend, as *kamptein* did in
Greek. Borrowed into colloquial Latin, it became *gamba,* a leg, the
thing that could bend. It became *gambolde* and *gambad* in Old French,
throwing one's legs around, and a particular sort of throwing one's
legs in English is *gambol.* Borrowed through Spanish it became *gambit,*
an opening move in chess. The Modern French form of leg, *jambe,*

was used figuratively in building and borrowed into English as *jamb,* as in *doorjamb.* It probably became confused with *gammelen,* a Germanic word meaning to play, and produced *gamble,* which was the easier, because, as we have seen, an intrusive /b/ comes naturally after /m/. Other borrowings have produced *gam,* a slang for leg, "especially a well-turned female leg," *gambado,* a leap in which a horse gets all four feet off the ground, and another use of *gambado* as a leg covering. Naturally, these meanings developed in part by normal mental processes within the various languages, as when the *jambe* that was a French leg became an upright post in construction, but most of the large shifts in meaning are to be associated with a new use in a new land. Such changes could be called *corruption* or *perversion,* as from some points of view they are, but such innuendoes imply that there is some reason for keeping terms unaltered. There is no such reason; the Greeks have every right to keep **kamp-* as a symbol meaning to bend if they want to, but that is no reason why the Romans should not use a similar form, *gamba,* to mean leg, wherever they got the suggestion. In so doing they harm no user of Greek and make Latin the richer.

Meanwhile, a combination of borrowing and compounding developed. The nineteenth and twentieth centuries saw the beginning of what we are now learning to call the "knowledge explosion." Science advanced, invention flourished. The world is now deluged, especially in the United States, but elsewhere as well, with new elements, new chemical compounds, newly discovered physical forces, new medicines, new philosophical concepts. Old English had supplied us few words for such things, and on the whole few terms exact enough to describe the innovations. We could not borrow terms; there was no place to borrow them from. Consider *monopropellant.* For this we might make a compound like the following composed of native words or early borrowings: *made-out-of-one-thing-or-not-many-things-closely-knit-so-that-the-way-you-get-the-drive-and-what-makes-something-go-are-both-to-gether-in-one-thing.* This would be a cumbersome term, and not even very accurate; why would it not serve as well for a horse that had just eaten some oats?

Fortunately, there was a ready solution. In the late eighteenth century, a brilliant Swede known as Carolus Linnaeus put the plant kingdom in order by cataloguing plants and describing them in Latin, producing the so-called Latin names. For example, many flowers have lilylike characteristics, but Linnaeus isolated a group of these, called them *lilium,* which he could do by describing their common characteristics. Then one of these could be called *lilium giganteum;* of course many lilies may be gigantic when compared with violets, but this was the largest lily, and by using the Latin modifier all other big lilylike things could be excluded. Again, *lilium lanceforum* could become a particular lily with a lancelike leaf, although most lilies have leaves that resemble spearheads. *Lilium tigrinum* could become a particular lily with spots like those of a tiger, although spotted flowers are not uncommon.

The idea spread. Similar systems were used to describe animals, mollusks, even wonder drugs—almost anything technical. Words like *antibiotics* and *mononucleosis* can be built up out of Latin and Greek syllables, and if the whole becomes clumsy it can be cut down so that *staphylococcus* becomes *staph* or *staf.* Such words spread internationally, with only minor differences in spelling and pronunciation; *antibiotic* in English is *antibiotique* in French. Doctors in much of the world have similar names for diseases and for the prescribed cures, the whole promoted by the fact that Greek and Latin derived from PIE, and that modern IE languages like English, French, and German are known to literate persons everywhere.

VERBAL HABITS OF THE AMERICANS

Two developments are notable in American English, compounding and the use of acronyms. The first was rampant in the eighteenth and nineteenth centuries. When immigrants came, and then turned into pioneers as they moved west, they encountered creatures enough like those they knew in the Old Country to be recognizable, but also recognizably different. Rabbits, for example, were indigenous in Europe, and the New World had rabbitlike creatures, but these rodents were clearly not the same. Consequently the newcomers used the European word as a generic term, and produced a new compound that described this particular sort of rabbit. A very common rodent with a bit of bobbing fluff became a *cotton-tail rabbit,* and soon a *cottontail.* A southern version became a *marsh rabbit,* and some larger species with long ears, the *jackass rabbit,* cut down to *jack rabbit,* and another subgroup that grows such long winter hair that its feet appear to be great pads, the *showshoe rabbit*. Of course this sort of thing has occurred in all new countries; South America produced the *rabbit-squirrel* and Australia the *rabbit-rat*. There were *rabbit-ear oysters, rabbit-mouth suckers,* and the *rabbit-mouth moth.*

Such compounding is an old device, but it bursts out anew whenever peoples move into new land—as it had burst out when Angles and Saxons moved into Celtic Britain—but it is declining now that Australia, Canada, and the United States are pretty well explored. More recently there has been another change in pattern; the newly discovered creatures today are likely to be microscopic, and users of microscopes are mostly not common people. If a scientist discovers an insect that grows its wings internally he does not call it an *inner-winged fly;* he calls it the same thing in Classical syllables, one of the *endopterygota.*

Another rash is notably American, the proliferation of acronyms—words made up of parts of words, especially initial letters. Some of these can be tongue-twistingly long, although shorter than the originals, like the initialism ADCOMSUBORDCOMPHIBSPAC for *Administrative Command, Subordinate Command, Amphibious Forces, Pacific Fleet.* Some acronyms become common; any child knows what ZIP code means, even if he does not recognize *zoning improvement plan* as the original of ZIP. Obviously, *ZIP* was intended to suggest the speed of *zip,* and the postal service has not been alone in choosing a name that would produce a suggestive acronym such as NOW, AIM, and SHAME. SCOOP is the term of a group that resents cleaning up after dog-walkers; they must have had the acronym in mind when they called themselves Stop Crapping on Our Premises. Such new terms now require a separate dictionary having tens of thousands of entries, and acronyms continue to multiply like rabbits (which as RABBITS might stand for Rodomontade Antiterseness Bureaucrats Busy Increasing Tautological Statistics, but has not yet done so).

We might consider what I have elsewhere called *novae* in the language, utilizing the figure of heavenly bodies that suddenly and even inexplicably flare up. Consider the word *state*. It comes to us from PIE through Latin, and became the common term for an autonomous country; Germany and France were called *states.* The name came to be applied to what were not autonomous political units, the British colonies in America, when these became parts of the United States. Now the word has flared up in dozens of derived uses and hundreds of compounds: *states rights, state capitol, state line, statewide, state's evidence, state aid, state bank, state park, state university, states-righters, states-rights Democrat.*

Meanwhile, a few verbal uses had developed, and one, some three centuries ago, concerned the use of words formally, as though in the name of a state. A document of 1641 includes the objection, "The question is not rightly stated in the Conclusion." Such uses continued, but sparsely; the *Oxford English Dictionary,* which cuts off at 1900, found relatively few occurrences. Then, almost suddenly, this use of the word blossomed like a nova in the sky. As far as I can recall, I did not use *state* as a verb when I was a child, but when I started to teach, twenty years later, I was horrified to find that my students looked upon *said* as a naughty four-letter word and used *stated* when they meant only that words had been emitted. Today these students are middle-aged adults, still writing and speaking *state* where my generation used *say;* their children, of course, use *state* as though the word *say* does not exist. Meanwhile, purists try to discourage the new use, calling it "loose," and publishers' editors hound it from published books, but *state* as a verb has become a nova in the language, although it shows no sign of fading back to obscurity as heavenly novae conveniently do.

Or consider *facility.* The word was first noticed in the sixteenth century; in 1531 the educator Sir Thomas Elyot recommended that children be "trayned with a pleasant faciliti"; as the *Oxford* dictionary defined the word it meant "the quality, fact, or condition of being easy or easily performed." That dictionary found no example of the word being used in its most common current American usage, and in fact at this writing no dictionary has recorded the word in the use implied in such locutions as "a correctional facility," "a facility for alcoholics," "adequate facilities for treatment." In this use, *facility* is not a "quality, fact, or condition" and has nothing to do with making something easy. It is a building, an office, a staff of trained personnel, a specialist, or some specialized provision. At a minimum it is something or somebody dedicated to a limited service, and this use is now so common in American English that within a few years it has grown to exceed all other uses of the word. Other terms that have undergone similar change include *phase* (as a noun and in the verbal phrase *phase out*), *development* (in the sense *real estate development*), *community* and *welfare* (in such phrases as *community welfare*), and a few hundred more involved in governmental and social problems.

One might notice an odd twist here. Most of these words come from Latin or Greek, albeit many of them through French. We have long borrowed such words to serve generalized purposes. *Transportation* may go back to sweating slaves and servants carrying loads on their backs, but we have employed the word for its general implications. *Inflammatory* may come from starting a fire, but it has taken on general and figurative uses.

In these recent American novae just the reverse has occurred. We have taken a generalized word that developed from the Classical tongues and have used it for something specific. *Facility* formerly meant—and still does in some occurrences—"ease of doing something," "lack of difficulty," but now usually it means a bureaucrat and his office, a doctor and his hospital *facilities*—one just cannot write American English any more without using these new concrete uses of an old abstract term.

WORDS OUT OF WORDS: PREFIXES AND SUFFIXES

Another means of evolving terminology combines several devices. A word or root, whether native or borrowed, can be given an affix, that is, a bound morpheme. Practically speaking, for English, such affixes are prefixes or suffixes. We have long had the word *able,* which a modern dictionary defines as "having enough power, skill, etc. to do something." We can make a negative of this by using a negative word with it, *not able.* Or, we can use a negative prefix and get the same result with one word, *unable.* Such terms have developed in unnumbered thousands, from *aback* to *zymurgy.* The affixes themselves are few in number, but they are omnipresent, powerful in their ability to shift and generate meaning, and curiously interknit because of their relations within the IE language family.

Most of these affixes are old words, or to phrase the same statement in another way, they are old free morphemes that in some uses have become bound morphemes. We have seen that the English prefix *for-* is a cognate of Latin *per-, pre-, par-,* and *pro-,* and that these all go back to an old root meaning to move or to be ahead as the result of moving. Similarly, prefixes like *un-* and some of those like *in-* go back to PIE **ne,* which is preserved in English as *no, not, nothing* (no thing), *naughty, never,* and many more, along with loan words from

Latin, *nulla* and *nil,* and Old High German *nix.* That is, **ne* was a negative; it survived into Middle English unchanged as a word: Chaucer, in saying that his Knight used no bad language, phrased his assertion in a triple negative including *ne* as "He *nevere* yet *no* vileynye *ne* sayde"—all three of the words I have italicized being from PIE **ne,* which meanwhile has become fruitful in affixes.

Prefixes from **ne* have come into Modern English both by direct descent and as several cognates through borrowing. The zero-grade combining form **n-* gives us *un-;* it is so common that any dictionary is likely to enter more than a thousand *un-* words, and compounds with it can readily be devised, even with new words, as in the *undefused bomb,* and *an unhippylike costume.* The same root has come into English through three different Latin forms: *non-,* still an actively combining form as in *nonnegotiable* and *nonwhite; neg-* as in *negate, renegade,* and even *deny,* although that takes a bit of explaining; and *in-,* which is perhaps as comomn as *un-,* although under many guises like *il-, im-,* and *ir-.*

To understand these we should recall the discussion of sound change, and that a sound may change because the shift from one nasal to another is difficult and uncommon in English and because /b/ is the stop corresponding to the nasal /m/. Another evidence of the same principle has operated with *in-;* it is preserved in words like *incompetent* and *inhospitable,* but adjacent to an /m/ it becomes another nasal as in *immature* and *immaculate,* and a similar change can occur before a corresponding stop as in *imbecile* and *impeccable.* Before an /r/ the /n/ may be absorbed into a consonant as in *irreverent* and *irrelevant;* it can become /l/ as in *illiterate, illogical.* It can even be absorbed within a vowel before palatals, as in *ignorant,* which means not knowing, because English *know* comes from **gno-,* as in *ignoramus.*

Likewise, words with prefixes cognate with *un-* can come from other IE languages. In Greek the prefix occurs as *a-* or *an-,* as in *amoral* and *anemia,* meaning respectively *not moral* and *no blood.* Even a few rare words have come in from Sanskirt, where the prefix took similar forms, as in *ahimsa,* meaning the noninjury to human life, and *amrita,* food for the gods, who are not mortal.

Now the plot thickens. PIE had another root similar in form to **ne,* formalized as **en,* but appearing also in both English and Latin as *in-.* In English it causes no confusion, because it is associated with the word *in* and contrasted in form with *un-.* But in Latin the two roots appear as the same forms, as *en-* or *in-;* the *in-* that means *not,* as in *indirect* and *impertinent,* cannot be distinguished from the *in-* form that means in or on as in *insert, immerse,* and *impel.* Furthermore, some of these words have developed almost opposite meanings, *invade* as against *impede, invoke* and *instruct* as against *inhibit* and *ignore.* Thus with *in-* or *en-* as prefixes the IE roots will not do much to determine meanings, but they will explain the confusion between the *in-* that means *not* and the *in-* that means *in, on, into,* or *onto.*

Prefixes can be handy, both in understanding and expressing oneself. Some affixes have limited and determinable uses; *anti-* means *against* and *ante-* means *before. Antiwar* means against war and *antebellum* means before the war; the two may become confused in people's minds, but they are never confused in careful usage and the meanings are so sure that anybody can use them to coin new words. The meanings of *anti-Hitler* and *anti–sex education* would be obvious at once, although they are not likely to appear in any dictionary.

Some combinations with affixes may not have an obvious and certain meaning. Consider *innocuous.* It means not harmful, but so far as its form reveals, it might be related to Latin *noctis,* thus meaning *not at night,* that is, by daylight, or it might mean going on into the night, and thus suggest something like *interminable.* Or it might be related to **nek-,* meaning death; thus *innocuous* would mean *undead* or *lively.* Or it might be derived from **negwhro-,* meaning a kidney, and thus a swimming pool could be *innocuous,* not kidney-shaped. This sort of thing could go on and on. But even so, affixes have their uses; if they do not always and infallibly reveal meaning, they do help one to remember meaning. Anyone who knows the word *noxious* will have little trouble remembering the meaning of *innocuous,* once he has learned it.

In fact, affixes are so handy that learning some of them deliberately is a helpful gesture; for most of them, looking up the etymology will help. One might notice that in English, prefixes are mainly concerned with meaning, suffixes with grammatical use.

PREFIXES

a-, an-, not, without; related to English *un-;* see above.

ab-, abs-, from, away from; related to English *of, off,* the /b/ of Latin being the voiced stop corresponding to /f/.

ac-, ad-, toward, to; related to English *at.*

ana-, ant-, anti-, back, opposite, against; related to English *and* as in *answer,* swear against.

co-, com-, con-, cum-, with, together; may be related to *gather, together, c* being the spelling of /k/, a voiceless stop, /g/ the corresponding voiced palatal.

de-, from, away, off; may be related to *to* and *too;* the same *du-, de-, del-,* or *d-* that appears in place-names and surnames like *Du Pont,* meaning from the bridge, and *Delcourte,* from the court.

di-, dif-, dis-, not, apart; Old English *to-, te-,* has been lost; OE *tobrecken* meant to break all to pieces.

for-, and *fore-,* various meanings, related to *par-, per-, pre-, pro-;* see discussion above.

e-, es-, ex-, former, out of; not in English, but can be remembered from words like *extra,* which formerly meant on the outside, *escape,* to get out.

en-, in-, both not and in; see above.

inter-, between; goes back to **en;* see above.

intra-, in, within; also goes back to **en,* but accords with English *in.*

mis, an English prefix, involving change, usually for the worse; appears also in English *mad.*

par-, per-, pre-, pro-, many uses, partly revealed through English *through;* see above.

re-, red-, back, again; may be related to a word meaning turn again, as in English *toward* (*to-weard, to* plus *turn*).

sub-, under, up from under; cognate with English *up.*

super-, upper, uppermost, highest; cognate with English *over,* formerly spelled *ofer,* Latin /p/ cognate with English /f/.

trans-, meaning through; cognate with English *through,* also with English *thirl,* as seen in *nostril,* a nose-hole.

under-, meaning about what *under* does as a word; cognate with *infernal* from Latin, referring to the lower depths.

SUFFIXES

-able, -ible, see above; the English form, *able* is likely to appear with English roots, and is the form most used in making new modifiers; *-ible* is used with many Classical roots, but not all.

-aceous, -acious, -itious, like, pertaining to; a Latin device for making modifiers out of other words, especially from nouns.

-age, a Latin device for making nouns, especially out of verbs.

-ance, -ence, another means of making nouns out of verbs; often names for action.

-ant, -ent, endings to make modifiers out of verbs.

-ation, -ition, a means of making nouns; usually there are corresponding verbs in English, *create, creation; define, definition.*

-dom, condition, quality, dominion; a native suffix related to *doom,* meaning judgment; formerly a formal sort of ending as in *kingdom,* but now used generally as in *officialdom.*

-hood, state, quality; another native means of making a noun, which has gone a long way from its earlier meaning of bright, shining.

-ise, -ize, cause, do, act, etc.; a Greek suffix to make verbs of nouns, it has come into English through Latin and French, and can now be used to turn almost any noun into a verb; related to *-ism.*

-ism, state, characteristic, doctrine; a Greek way of making nouns, that has come through Latin, sometimes French; related to *-ize.*

-ment, manner, quality, means; a Latin means of making abstract verbs into nouns.

-ness, condition of being; a Germanic way of making abstract nouns.

-ous, -ious, -eous, full of, having the quality of; from a Latin way of making adjectives.

-ship, skill, art, condition; related to English *shape* and to many words involving the idea of shaping, especially by cutting; not related to the English word *ship.*

-sion, -tion, action, process, outcome; a noun-forming device using the past participle of Latin verbs.

-tude, that which is, state of being; from a Latin suffix to make abstract nouns out of modifiers.

-ure, process, act; a Latin means of indicating the result of an action.

So now we can return to our original question: Why do languages grow? Apparently they grow because the users of the language have new uses for it, particularly new counters for meaning. And when a language needs new terms, there are several places to get them. No doubt most languages use most of these devices most of the time, although fashions may shift—as Old English used compounding extensively, Middle English borrowing, and then American English turned once more to compounding, only to turn away from the practice as the society matured. The readiest way, sometimes, is to borrow terms from another language. Or established words can be used for new purposes, relying on such familiar mental processes as generalization and specialization, and these established words may be either native elements or linguistic bits previously borrowed—words are like human beings in this, that after a short time the immigrants may be treated very much like the natives. Or linguistic units may be combined. Some of these combinations may be what we have called compounds, just words stuck together, like *houseboat* and *boathouse,* but others involve old words that have become affixes. In fact, a language needing words for work may even utilize those devised for play—but that is another matter, to be dealt with in the next chapter.

9

LANGUAGE
TO PLAY WITH,
INCLUDING SLANG

LANGUAGE LEARNING

Our Puritan ancestors may be to blame. They warned that "In Adam's Fall we sinned all," and were aware that for eating exotic food and having dealings with a serpentine fellow, Adam and Eve were evicted and punished by having to work: "In the sweat of thy face shalt thou eat bread." The descendants of the Puritans admonished one another, "Work for the night is coming." Or perhaps the national ethic was encouraged by the centuries when there was always a frontier, where living was hard, where parents taught their offspring, "Early to bed and early to rise . . ." "Plow deep while sluggards sleep . . ." One vigorous gentleman is said regularly to have roused his sons on Monday, "Get up, boys. Four-thirty of a Monday morning. Tomorrow's Tuesday. Next day, Wednesday. Half the week gone, and nothing done." The emphasis was on work; even a modest meliorative like "All work and no play" assumes that most of the time will be given to work. Work was good; leisure and fun, if not quite blameworthy, were at least suspect and to be indulged with restraint. In the view of many they were positively bad, as in "The Devil finds work for idle hands to do."

It may not be so. Civilization seems to have grown at least as much from the spirit of fun as from the obligation to labor. True, fun may not sport itself on an empty stomach, and part of man's civilization sprang from easier ways to get enough to eat, planting seeds and prying mussels off rocks, but after immediate creature needs were satisfied, culture may have grown more with laughing than with sweating. At worst the ne'er-do-well—if he was such—who wanted to spend his time with wine, a woman, and a book of verses "underneath the bough" was doing less to disrupt the ecology than does a strip miner with a bulldozer. Mother England seems to have understood these matters better than have her colonies; the great English public schools like Eaton and Harrow, the universities like Cambridge and Oxford, were calculated to produce an elite, an elite that was to supply the governmental leaders, the social arbiters, the moral and artistic creators. And the elite was produced at least as much by play as by work.

FUN WITH THE BODY

But whatever the social rewards of play, the spirit of fun has been too little praised as a begetter of language. We have seen that language responds to a need, and one can so define fun—indeed it may be one. High spirits promote both the generation and the preservation of speech. Consider the fun man has had with the figurative use of his own body: the *body* of a work, by the *skin* of one's teeth, to *foot* a bill, the *mouth* of a river, an *arm* of the sea, the *finger* of scorn, a *blood* bath, the *eye* of a hurricane, an *ear* of corn, to *hand* over, an *elbow* joint, to *knuckle* down, to have a *stomach* for a venture, to have a *heart,* the *bowels* of compassion, a bare*bones* budget, to *toe* the mark, to be a *heel,* to *shoulder* a burden, a *nose* for news, a chair *back,* a *hair*-raising scream, a bottle*neck, knee*bend, a shout at the top of one's *lungs, kidney* bean, *liver*wort, put *teeth* into a law, to get something off one's *chest* by making a clean *breast* of it. And these omit the supposedly delicate terms associated with copulation and excretion, which from time immemorial have been potent begetters of linguistic amusement.

One of the body parts the most fertile in fun is the globelike object that tops the human torso, in English the *head.* Even before men discovered that the brains are the seat of intelligence, man's domelike skull was the subject of figurative play, and thereafter the idea that the brain-space was actually empty or solid bone became one of man's pet sources of humor. This sort of thing goes back as far as we can trace language. In fact, the Indo-European root, *kaput-* is under suspicion of involving a figure, even a joke; it probably derives from *keu-*, which has given us words like *cup* and *cupola,* and may have meant an empty, bowl-like object. (For English /h/ from IE /k/, English /d/ from IE /t/, see Chapter 6.) Figurative uses began early; the *capitol* from Latin is the head of state, a *capital* the head city, a *capital letter* the head letter, a *chapter* something that had a heading. Through Old French the Latin word for head became *cabbage,* so that *cabbage head* is merely *head-head;* through Spanish a cognate designates a *cabezon,* a fish named for its big head. A *cape* into the sea was a *head*land, which could also be called a *head.* To *head for* some place meant to turn one's head in that direction. Similarly, a boat can *make head;* a man can have a *head* for figures, be *head* over heels in debt or in love, or he can lose his *head,* have his *head* turned, or several persons can put their *heads* together—there are dozens. Meanwhile, a head could be called a *brain pan,* or just a *pan* as it was in the oath, *by my pan,* with *pan* in its literal sense meaning about what it does in *tin pan.* Likewise *skull* became a name for the head, probably from Scandinavian, but we do not know whether *skull* came first as a word for a beaker and became figuratively a head, or whether men drank out of human skulls and then used the word figuratively for a cup. And *pate,* of uncertain origin, probably referred to a flattish vessel, the word possibly a variant form of *plate.* Even the anatomical term for a head involves some figurative use; *cranium* is related to *horn,* possibly because horns sprung from the head, but more likely because both were shell-like bony parts. A head became one's *dome,* another roundish, empty object.

With the growing knowledge of what brains are good for, the joke increased that for humorous purposes the head is solid. One of the terms may have gotten started because there were *head-blocks,* used in fitting hats, and by Shakespeare's time a playwright could refer to "blockheads and stupid asses." There were various ways of saying that a person's head was made from a block of wood, a *woodenhead, wooden-headed, square-headed; loggerhead* is related to *log.* Obviously one of the best insults would imply that the head is solid bone, and once *bonehead* had been developed, one could be *boneheaded* and perform *bonehead* acts. Soon one could make a *boner,* and to study one could *bone up* a subject. Other solid objects could be called upon;

a head could be a *melon* or a *bean,* the latter apparently from baseball, where *bean* developed *beanball,* a pitch deliberately thrown at the head. *Coconuts* provided an obvious comparison, along with nuts of all sorts; Chaucer says a man had a "not-head," but whether he meant *nut-head, knot-head,* or what is not clear. Hundreds of solid or empty objects have become slang for the head: *attic, belfry, billiard ball, biscuit, cabbage, cavity, filbert, gable, gourd,* and on through *upper story* and *weak end.*

FUN WITH SOUND AND SENSE

Speakers have had fun with the sound as well as sense. Happy combinations involving rhyme or alliteration—and sometimes both—have lived longer and spread wider because of a repetition of sound, as in *shilly-shally, rough and tough, hurdy-gurdy, boogie-woogie, the heeby-jeebies, weasel words, paper profits, neither rhyme nor reason, children and chicken must always be pickin', jet set, gang-bang, fender-bender, Dirty Gertie from Bizerte, large as life, leave in the lurch, make mountains out of molehills,* even *Boston brown bread* and *baked beans.* Playing with both sense and sounds can be involved in various sorts of puns; Mary McCarthy twitted "certain critics" with having got the knack of always "striking when the irony is hot." Our fathers were amused that "great aches from little toe corns grow."

Perhaps the most famous pun is attributed to Charles Lamb, along with some others. Lamb had a resounding reputation as a punster, and doubtless to embarrass him, since being humorous on order is usually impossible, a slow-witted fellow guest demanded that Lamb produce a pun on the spot. Lamb, a gentle man, inquired politely, "U-pun what subject?" The questioner missed that one, but aware that he had to think fast, blurted, "The king." Lamb demurred, saying, "The king is not a subject." Many scoffers derogate puns—and indeed some can be pretty obvious—but Edgar Allan Poe may have had a point when he remarked that persons who dislike puns are those "least able to utter them." The German satirist Lichtenberg may have had an even better point when he observed, "Where the common people like puns, and make them, the nation is on a high level of culture." Even though puns are bad, punning seems to be good, probably for the pun-prone mind and certainly for the pun-ept language.

On a more sober and artistic level, sound enters into rhetoric and rhetoric cultures language. Rhetoric is not all fun, but clearly some linguistic growth stems from the pleasure that springs from turning a phrase well, of providing a charming setting for a scintillating idea, and of discovering such phrases when they have been well-turned. Doubtless many minds—one of them was that of President Kennedy's speech writer—toyed with the injunction, "Ask not what your country can do for you; ask rather what you can do for your country." Lincoln, jolting his way toward the cemetery at Gettysburg and scribbling notes, must have taken satisfaction in the sequence "a government of the people, by the people, for the people," and thousands of orators have since seized upon the phrase. Countless apt phrasings have thriven by their aptness: "to be or not to be," "methinks the lady doth protest too much," "more honored in the breach than in the observance." Somebody happened upon such a pleasant expression as "a one-woman war," "a one-woman campaign," and in the subsequent decades there have been dozens of "one-woman" witticisms. Humor helps; an inoffensive carnivore in the southwestern United States was called a *ringtailed cat,* but he has now acquired a more attractive name, a Nahuatl term that means *half a mountain lion.* Wit and humor have helped even in the graveyard; several bereaved husbands are said to have had the following couplet inscribed on the uxorial headstone:

> Almighty God, to please His pallate,
> Has ta'en my Lettys to make His salate.

Lettys is of course a pun on *lettuce,* and *salate* represents an archaic pronunciation of *salad.* Somewhat more subtle is the following:

> One stone sufficeth—lo! what Death can do—
> Her who in life was not content with two.

Of course much-used phrases can become hackneyed. Smalltime politicians seem especially prone to such abuses; they fear that actions will *backfire* or *boomerang.* They *mend fences* at the *grass-roots level* while *keeping an ear to the ground.* They *lay the cards on the table, study the handwriting on the wall, keep the door open,* and try if necessary to *get off the hook.* They caution about *two-way streets,* or conversely about *one-way streets.* They praise *hitting nails on the head* but decry *hitting below the belt.* They warn against *opening Pandora's boxes, swapping horses in the middle of a stream, crossing bridges before one gets to them, killing geese that lay golden eggs, dragging red herrings across trails, sweeping things under the rug, hiding one's head ostrichlike in the sand, rocking the boat,* and *throwing the baby out with the bath.* Such people love figures out of sports; they *get on the ball,* believe in being *one of the team,* and avoid being *benched* or *sent to the sidelines* or *having two strikes against one.* All sorts of persons, perhaps especially those who have more need to speak pompously than wealth of words and ideas to speak with, love such figures, and apparently gain self-confidence and self-satisfaction from them. The late senator Joseph McCarthy became known for his outraged protest, "That's the most unheard of thing I ever heard of." And even hearers who abhor figurative jumblings must recognize that the language is colored by them, if not made more colorful through them.

THE SLANGUAGE INSTINCT

Many people have tried, more or less seriously, to define slang:

Slang is language that takes off its coat, spits on its hands, and goes to work.

Slang is the hobo of language; here today and gone tomorrow, leaving behind the stale odor of cheap hangovers, of unwashed castoff clothing, of better days.

Slang fixes into portable shape the nebulous ideas of the vulgar.

Correct English is the slang of prigs who write history and essays. And the strongest slang of all is the slang of poets.

Slang loosens its necktie, elevates its nonchalant feet, and prepares for a good bellylaugh.

Slang is the push-button elevator of language; it may get you a little way in a hurry, without exercising either your brain or the legs you stand on.

Slang is the speech of him who robs the literary garbage carts on their way to the dumps.

Slang is Puck in pasture, the bastard of the immortal imp in man.

Slang is dull; the best thing about it is that it is no worse.

A people who are prosperous and happy, optimistic and progressive, will produce much slang.

Slang is the language of street humor, of fast, high, and low life. Jive talk, Man. It's cool, ain't it?

Slang is a conventional tongue with many dialects, which are as a rule unintelligible to outsiders.

Slang is the body of words and expressions frequently used by or intelligible to a rather large portion of the general public, but not accepted as good, formal usage by the majority.

The fact is that slang is easier to spot, or to invent, than to define— the last definition above, abridged from Stuart Berg Flexner in *Dictionary of American Slang* (1960), is less fun but more factual than most of the others. Slang is mainly use; most slang expressions are not vocabulary items developed by slang-users for slang needs; they are standard terms turned to slangy practices. *Broad* was an adjective in good standing before it became a slang noun for a woman who is not.

Everybody believes he knows slang when he hears it, but few can agree as to its nature or its impact, any more than the worthies quoted above could agree. Many parents detest it and try to scour it from their offspring; some teenagers flaunt it, a badge of their revolt, a certificate of their being *in*, or *hip*, or *groovy*, or whatever the slang has become when this sentence is printed. Teachers may try to restrain it, either on the theory that it is cheap and "bad language drives out good" or because some students use it for all purposes, and most slang is neither stable nor precise. Scholars and writers may delight in it, finding it one of the humbly creative parts of the language, what they call "interesting." Editorializers may hear in it the death rattle of culture, taste, and even intelligence.

At worst one can observe that slang is a way of having fun with language, perhaps not very much fun in most instances, but widespread fun, fun that requires so little by way of wit or wisdom in its users that the most mentally disadvantaged can make something of it. At its best it is a lively and harmless sport. It can be cruel, of course; a wife probably does not like to be called a *ball and chain;* doubtless a serious psychiatrist, concerned with the tragedies of his patients, would prefer some other epithet than *headshrinker*. But slang provides more good clean fun than do most human antics, and for more people.

In America, one of the famous bodies of slang was the "tall talk" attributed to "ringtailed roarers," the broad-horning Mike Finks and backwoodsy politicans like Davy Crockett. They were said to be the *real screamers, half hoss and half alligator* (or *snapping turtle*, depending on the roarer) and a touch of the *airthquake* who refused milk before their eyes were opened and *called out for a bottle of Rye*, who *would live forever and then turn to a whiteoak post*. With or without provocation they would *teetotaciously exflunctiate* you or *ramsquaddle* you *bodaciously*. In the unlikely event of any *conbobberation* with legal minions, such a roarer could always *absquatulate* or *jumsecute elegantiferously*, riding a streak of lightning if necessary and leaving the *snollygoster obfusticated*. I have elsewhere tried to show that the broadhorning Finks and Little Johnny Earthquakes of the frontier did not command such Latinisms, that the fad provided a pleasant way for a bored journalist to fill his columns and while away an idle hour, but however that may be, the talk stems one way or another from somebody having fun.

Much of the objection to slang rises not from slang at all, but from fuzzy definition. To many people slang is whatever they do not like in language; they may include nonstandard usage in their denigration of slang, words like *ain't* and *thunk* or terms supposedly vulgar. Such questions will be considered under *usage* in Chapter 11. And slang can be deadly dull; a mother who hears her child label everything from the new girl in school to the new flavor in ice cream with a single meaningless adjective may have reason to despair. She may wonder what this refusal to use the language with any discrimination is doing to her darling's mind; or she may be bored by hearing for the thousandth time a bit of cuteness that was not very funny after the fifth.

Notable in slang are its limits. Language, as we have seen, must be infinitely expandable, adequate to anything that its users can think. Slang provides almost none of the grammatical machinery with which language works, and it is so restricted in terminology that for most subjects it has nothing, not even names. There are plentiful terms for girls, especially for seductive girls, or for the sexual potentials of girls, but few for wives and mothers who happen to be nice people. Sports, especially spectator sports, glory in slang, but very few slang terms spring from manufacturing or accounting. Food, and of course inebriating drink, generate slang and provide words that can be used for figurative purposes—*bread, peach, tenderloin, tomato, lemon, corn*— but science provides little slang. The underworld is a source of slang; the *mob* must have its *gorillas* to fill the *meat wagon*. At the moment slang flows from the drug culture with its *dopeheads, hopheads, acid-*

heads, and *cokeheads.* Slang is picturesque, although it provides a limited picture.

Curiously, slang is both more enduring and more transient than is commonly supposed. A popular notion is that a slang expression, the happy inspiration of some unsung genius, sweeps to popularity. It may then become standard speech, or may pine away. Both of these happen, of course, but neither happens as frequently as is often supposed. Most slang expressions never travel far or last long. Slang that gains wide currency is likely to remain slang, at least for a long time. To *pipe down* is more than a hundred years old, and is probably about as slangy and about as respectable as it was when Melville used it in *White Jacket;* people have been poking other people in the *snoot* for a century. To *bust a gut* and to *butt in* are old phrases. The upshot is that one can thumb through many pages of a slang dictionary before he finds any locution that has become standard English. Some slang relies on sound—*nice-Nelly, rinky-dink, honky-tonk;* such terms may linger on, but their sound alone is not enough to commend them for long, and while they last they endure as slang. Much picturesque use relies on figures of speech; whether a *ham-and-egger* is an indistinguishable citizen or a pugilist who can barely make a living, the basis of the slang is figurative, and the use can slip out of the language leaving little trace behind. Some slang does survive of course; we have seen that figurative terms for the head have survived, and they must once have been slang terms. But for every word like *skull* or *dome* that lived, dozens died.

FUN AND LANGUAGE LEARNING

Perhaps I may recount my own observations. One of my grandchildren, Hanna, was old enough to toddle, but not old enough to talk. When I came to visit she would seize me and start babbling. Assuming that this was fun for her, I babbled back, except that not being an accomplished babbler I adopted some subject for a conversation and talked in words and sentences. Soon I discovered that this exchange was indeed a conversation, that while I was asking questions and giving answers, so was Hanna, although I knew the subject of my conversational sallies and I assume she had none. With that I began to listen to the patterns in her babbling, the stresses, pitches, tones, and junctures. I soon concluded that she was using all the sentence patterns she could be expected to hear very often in her household, although using babble-sounds to fill up the grammatical patterns. Apparently she thought this was what adults did, and she was having fun playing at being an adult.

This babbling of Hanna's had linguistic interest. She was learning speech patterns by imitation, and speech patterns provide the device with which human beings reveal syntax. The assumption had long been that children learn words during the second year of their lives and then begin to find grammatical means to put them together, starting about the third year. But here was an infant who as yet knew no words, but had already laid the foundation for learning English grammar by mimicking English sentence patterns. Furthermore, she was practicing the patterns so much that they had become second nature to her, and all this before she could speak a word. I have since learned that she was not unusual in this, that many children babble in sentence patterns. Perhaps all babblers do, although some children, for whatever reason, never babble much—and that may be one reason some of them are slow learning to speak.

As soon as Hanna acquired a few words she had fresh material for games. Doubtless her older sisters started it by pointing to a picture in a magazine or catalogue and saying, "What's that, Hanna?" If Hanna knew, she would answer; if not the sister would tell her. This exchange was intended to be a lesson in vocabulary, but Hanna soon took it over and made a game of it. She would point and say "Whazzat!" After a few identifications it would be the adult's turn to ask "What's that?" and Hanna would gleefully shout "Daddy," "Fishie," "Kitty," "Clock," or whatever was appropriate. Apparently the essence of the game was speed; she delighted in getting the word out the instant the finger pointed. She would do this by the hour if she could get an adult to play the game with her, and of course unconsciously she was learning words and learning to control her tongue.

She developed other games, some involving rituals. In her home was an antique rocking chair, which would readily tip over backward, dumping a frightened Hanna on the floor. This chair delighted her; apparently she thought it was playing a game with her, trying to dump her out, while she tried to crawl into it without being dumped. Hanna's mother, with visions of concussions and broken bones, did not approve such scramblings, but she realized she could not forbid

Hanna to sit in a chair that others used. Accordingly, when Hanna was trying to squirm up into the rocker her mother would say "Careful," in a warning voice. Hanna was not being careful; presumably she did not know the meaning of *careful*. Her face was beaming with glee and prospective triumph, but she would repeat "Careful," using her mother's pitch patterns quite precisely. Apparently *careful* with the proper intonation was a sort of ritual, maybe even a charm against being dumped. Whatever it was, she was learning language, and learning it as part of having fun. Similarly, she had ritual speeches to be used when she fell down, and the like.

On the other hand, she did not learn when she was unhappy. If she was scolded or punished, she would shut out the world by hiding her face in the rug. There would be no play then for a long time, and little use of language.

All this has implications. Learning speech is an exacting job, but children master it. How they learn we do not know, but we do know that children have very different learning rates. Those that learn fast may be the bright ones, but within limits they may also be the lucky ones, those born into homes where they are not frightened by family quarreling, where people will play with them, and where they are allowed to babble interminably. More than anything else they may be the children who have learned how to have fun, for apparently having fun will usually include having fun with language. And later in life one good reason for studying etymology may be that it is a way to have fun with language. Conversely, parents who correct their children's usage may be doing more harm than good; in trying to promote correct usage they have stopped all learning of language by stopping the fun.

Most slogans probably do not do much good, but if there is one that should hang on the walls of all English classrooms it might be this: HAVE FUN.

10

LANGUAGE
WORKING IN ITS OWN WAY

DIALECTS

You speak a dialect.

To this, you may have had any of several reactions, including the following:

(Resentful) "I do not!"

(Trying to be polite and tolerant) "Perhaps. But I shouldn't really say it is that bad."

(Disturbed but trying to make the best of it) "I guess so. I never was good in English."

(Long-suffering and humble) "I know. But I'm working on it. It isn't as bad as it was."

(Nonchalant) "Of course."

(Objective and bored) "And I trust you understand that unless I speak a dialect I will not speak at all?"

Probably the best answer—because the statement is trivial—is the next to the last, and the last gives the best reason. The first four are the most likely answers, however, and in different ways each suggests a major misunderstanding or a minor tragedy. The fact is that dialects are indigenous to language and thus inevitable in man; a language that does not develop dialects would be as abnormal as a human being who cannot sweat—and neither would live long. Or to put it another way, dialects become the way languages work—no dialects, no language; no dialect speakers, no users of language. Part of the difficulty is that for many people, *dialect* is a seven-letter word, correspondingly worse than a four-letter word.

Dialect, like most common words, has several uses. People learning a second language almost always speak it badly. Japanese speakers learning English usually confuse /r/ and /l/; French and German natives will have trouble with /ð/ and /θ/, and are likely to use either /d/ or /z/. What they produce may be called *broken English,* but it can also be called a dialect. Similarly, a boy born in an illiterate home in a community where mostly ignorant people live will speak a dialect. Thus people who think of a dialect as something to be avoided or cured are using the term to describe careless, untutored, or nonstandard speech. But as a student of language uses the word *dialect,* and as nonspecialists are learning to use it, the boy who is the son of a doctor, who grows up in a cultured community and attends the best schools, also speaks a dialect. So does his father. So does his mother, even though she may have been a speech teacher, is an admired actress, or a social leader. That is, in this sense everybody speaks a dialect, or several of them, and nobody need be ashamed of his.

Naturally some dialects are more useful, more admired, or more fashionable than others. The doctor mentioned in the last paragraph would speak several dialects, of which one would include technical terms for diseases, medicines, and the appurtenances of his profession. Without this body of speech he could not practice; he could not converse with his fellow doctors, could not read professional journals, probably could not even think with the necessary precision. Similarly, if a ghetto boy becomes a doctor, he may not have to unlearn the unfashionable dialect he acquired from his parents and the neighboring hoodlums but he had best be careful where and when he uses it —it might even save his life if he is mugged, but it will cost him patients if he uses it in his office and damage his standing if he uses it at a professional meeting. Thus the question is not, do you speak a dialect, but do you speak the kind of dialects you want?

An artificial language could exist without dialects. No doubt when Esperanto was new it had only one dialect—it had only one speaker, the inventor, L. L. Zamenhof, and he could presumably have taught it to his family so exactly that their individual differences would not be called dialects. But it could not spread far or last long without differences developing, differences that would fall into patterns. Esperanto, in spite of its well-wishers, has not found any large role in modern society, and linguists doubt that it ever will. They surmise that no artificial language ever can, but if one does, the more it grows the more it will develop dialects. Nobody knows, as yet, how much American Sign Language is a language and how much it is a signal system to express natural languages, but one reason to believe that it is a language, or is becoming a language, is that it is growing dialects.

THE EGO AND THE IDIOLECT

Languages must live by dialects, because languages grow by and through minds, and minds work in ways that produce dialects. Consider an infant. He is very much like other infants, but not exactly like them. In fact, we have to believe that no other infant ever was or ever will embody quite the composition that coalesces in him, and this uniqueness incorporates an aptness, something we might call a language sense, and this, too, is different from the language sense of any other child, presumably even of an "identical" twin. From the moment of his birth he has experiences, and once more these will differ from all other experiences, at least to some degree, and for most human beings such transforming influences will go on for years, with infinite variations. One of these experiences is language; the result is that every human being has his unique use of language, what we call his *idiolect*.

An idiolect is such a grab bag as not even a kleptomaniac pack rat could accumulate. It is highly personal, and hence it can be discussed best in a personal way, since only the user of an idiolect will know it well enough. Here are some of my idiosyncracies. I use the word *pesky:* I became charmed while quite young with the way my mother said, "That pesky cat," when kitchen-brooming the offender, but I have never heard anybody except my mother and me say *pesky*. In the small town in which I grew up I played with the children of many families, including offspring of the town dullard, whose family all talked with a sort of whine. We amused ourselves by imitating the speech of these unfortunates, and later, when I tried to learn French nasals, I imagine I did it better for my childhood experience of trying to imitate the

dullard's twang. On a boat, returning after a year in England, I encountered a fellow midwesterner, who showed me an iridescent bowl
she had bought. I knew she considered it a great bargain and would
be glad to boast of how little it had cost. I asked her; she thought a
minute and translated the sum into pounds and shillings for me. So
much had happened to me in a year that a native American could no
longer recognize my native speech. These are only random bits out of
the infinity of everyone's linguistic experience, but even these few had
never been combined before and never will again—times have changed.

Thus in part one's idiolect results from his idiosyncrasies, but even
more it reflects dialects. Everybody lives in a certain home or a sequence
of homes, and in each of these places speech habits will have crystallized. If one grows up in Iowa he is likely to pronounce *aunt* to rhyme
with *pant,* but if he is native in New England it is more likely to
rhyme with *font, want,* or *taunt.* That is, he is learning a regional
dialect. And regional dialects are inevitable; language is always changing, and if groups of speakers are isolated in two places, the language
will change in one place differently from the way it changes in the
other place. Recently a new language was discovered in Alaska; it had
only some 250 speakers, but it was fragmented into dialects; when the
next Indian language is discovered on the upper Amazon River, it is
likely to contain dialects. At least, if its speakers have been segregated
long enough to develop a language, the language will have developed
dialects, and the chances are that some of these will have survived.

Or to put this more pertinently, English is not Dutch or German
because West Germanic speakers moved to the island of Britain and
lived somewhat isolated for hundreds of years; the insular Germanic
dialects grew in their own ways and the Continental Germanic dialects
grew in other ways. After some centuries, what had once been different
dialects had grown into different languages.

That is, the same sort of growth that assured for each of us an idiolect
has fathered dialects and has grandfathered languages. The change is
continuous, but for convenience we can recognize three stages that
result from the inevitable differentiation through language. Changes
in human beings and in language use determine that each of us will
speak an idiolect. The same sort of change, accompanied by standardization, will determine that there will always be bodies of speakers who
differ as groups from other bodies of speakers, although the two can
understand each other. We say they speak different dialects. If the

speakers of a dialect are isolated long enough, their speech will diverge so much that a native of one group will no longer understand a native of the other. We say they speak different languages—which in turn will by now be composed of dialects, and will be generating new idiolects. Actually, the distinction between languages and dialects is not so sharp as these definitions suggest. In our somewhat illogical world, politics and other considerations become involved in linguistic terms, and thus Danish and Norwegian, called languages, are not so different as some bodies of Chinese speech called dialects, but the distinctions are revealing if not precise.

Thus geographical dialects are the result of relative isolation in space. But land and sea are not the only isolaters. An employer and employee may never exchange a word, although they work in the same establishment for years. The garbage collector comes every week, but the garbage may be all that he and an apartment dweller are aware of having in common. Accordingly, there are social dialects as well as regional dialects, even occupational dialects, and for the lives of most of us the dialects that spring from society are the most important. If a cultured Philadelphian hears someone say *you-all,* he will assume that the speaker has lived somewhat to the south, but his estimate of the person is not likely to be much altered; he may even be intrigued. Similarly, if he hears someone pronounce *you* as /jiu/, with an in-glide before the vowel, he will assume that the speaker comes from farther north. But if he hears someone say *we-uns,* he will probably assume that the speaker is illiterate—he may be wrong, but that is another question— with whatever reservations he has for illiterates.

Dialects, although they consist only of standardization of linguistic quirks and habits, can be fun to observe and dreadfully important to deal with. First to the fun.

DIALECTS IN A NEW WORLD

If you were to start north from Florida, you might be surprised, unless you had lived long in the area, to notice how many people say *Do he?* and *He do* where you would use *does.* About the time you get to Chesapeake Bay you would stop hearing this use, and if you are perceptive, you might recall that you had heard people saying *It wasn't me,* with *wasn't* pronounced either /wɑnt/ or /wɔnt/. You had also heard them say *gwine* where you say *going*. And now you realize there have been other changes; the pitch of voices is different, even the sentence patterns have altered. That is, you have passed from one regional dialect area into another.

The new dialect area will last until you get to New York. You will hear people saying *door* with an /r/, whereas farther south it had been /doʊ/, /doə/, or /do/. In New York City itself you will find highly characteristic speech, pronunciation you associate with the Bronx, eastern Manhattan, and parts of Brooklyn—*Oil's goil* for *Earl's girl*—and *water*, said with an initial long *oo-* sound /uɔtə/. Once you are well into Connecticut you will hear a third body of dialects; *door* is now likely to be /dɔə/ or /dɑə/, more like the pronunciation in Virginia than that in New Jersey but still different. In fact, you may notice that many individual words are spoken rather like the way you had heard them in the far south, but that the tone of the voice and the speech rhythms are such that the total effect does not suggest the south at all. And this new set of dialectal patterns is likely to follow you, with some changes, all the way to the border of Maine, where in New Brunswick and Nova Scotia will be other dialects.

Now, if you wish, you could support these dialectal cleavages with thousands of details. You might notice that south of Pennsylvania and Delaware you could hear *I taken it, I heern it, What make him do that? I holp myself,* and *I might could.* In the north you could hear *He et* rather than *He ate, hadn't ought* rather than *ought not, see* as a preterite, *I be* rather than *I am,* although farther south you could have heard *be* as future, as in *I be dog* (*I'll be doggoned*). In the Midlands you could have heard *seen* as well as *saw* as a preterite, *clumb* along with *climbed, boilt* rather than *boiled,* and if you were bitten by a dog you could have been *dogbit.*

You could discover minor dialect areas, within these or breaking across them. Consider the word *bull.* It designates a common farm animal, but perhaps for reasons of modesty many other words have been used to designate the creature. In Connecticut and Massachusetts it is often a *sire.* Up into Vermont and New Hampshire one can hear *top cow, top ox, top steer,* and *critter,* which last is common also in Rhode Island. *Male cow* can be added in Pennsylvania, although such terms are rarer there. In the South a whole different range of terms appears; along the coast from Virginia south are *beast, male beast,* and *stock beast.* To the west, toward the mountains, are *brute, male brute,* and *stock brute*. The Chesapeake Bay area and valleys to the west prefer *male cow, ox,* and *steer*. There are even patches having *masculine* (rhymes with *mine*), in southern West Virginia and on islands off Massachusetts.

Such evidence is hard to classify and interpret. Dialects are easy to hear, but elusive to describe. Anybody who has been in Boston, Brooklyn, Philadelphia, and Charleston knows that the speech in each of these differs from all the others, but describing the differences is not easy. And it was much harder, a few decades ago, before we had *linguistic geography*. Anyone can notice that some Texas speakers pronounce *idea* as though it were spelled *oddy* /ɑdi/, whereas some Boston speakers say it as they would *eye-dear* /ajdijr/, but what is the spread of these pronunciations, socially and spatially? More important, what is the whole complex of vocabulary, pronunciation, usage, and grammar that distinguishes Boston Back Bay from the Texas panhandle? Linguistic geography provides something approaching a scientific tool for the study of such problems.

The method is a sampling device, using either interviewers or questionnaires. Someone who knows the nature of language and is acquainted with local dialects picks key locutions that spread irregularly. These may be verb forms—in a later chapter we shall have to raise the questions as to why verbs are aberrant in English. Or they may be calls to bring farm animals—*co-boss, chickie-chickie, sook* and *souie,* or whatever. Such terms are likely to be Americanisms and local. Animals were not much called in England; they were confined with hedges. Or the useful terms may be words occasioned by new sorts of farming, like *corncrib, crib house, corn house, corn stack;* maize did not grow in England. The linguist selects a few highly revealing terms of this sort, collects data about them in a controlled way, so that when the results are assembled on maps or are tabulated, patterns of language appear. For example, if you draw lines plotting the most northerly consistent occurrence of the verb forms I listed on a previous page, you will find you have line after line running from Chesapeake Bay west and southwest. Farther north similar plotting would produce lines running west from southern Connecticut. Here, then, you have the major dialect regions of the eastern coast of the United States.

Dialects were carried west. We can understand why people in eastern Kentucky and Tennessee speak as they do; their ancestors came west through Cumberland Gap and other openings in the mountains, bringing the dialectal patterns of western Virginia and North Carolina. Their speech differs from that of people in Mississippi and Alabama, because the plantation speakers moved south around the mountains to the delta lands along the gulf. Farther north, natives of New England and New York can be traced by their northern forms to Cleveland and Chicago, while the Midlanders from Pennsylvania tended to work down the Mississippi River. And so it went; the westering streams of dialect tended somewhat to blend as new migrants poured in, but much was preserved and can still be traced. Even today, pockets of northern speech can be found in and near San Francisco, attesting to the New Englanders who came by boat as part of the Gold Rush, and to a degree remained distinct from Midlanders from Pennsylvania and New Jersey, who had become Midwesterners, and who had later found their way across the great plains and the mountains.

THE AMERICANS IMPORT DIALECTS

Thus in part American English reflects American origins, some of which reach deep into the past. We have seen that Germanic dialects, forms of languages that descend from the Proto-Indo-Europeans, built up along the North Sea. One body of these West-Germanic speakers, called Angles, sailed west and occupied the eastern portion of the island of Britain, roughly from the mouth of the Thames to Scotland— the tough Scots and Picts were able for centuries to keep Germanic speakers out of the Celtic mountains as they had kept the Romans out. Another group, mainly Saxons, skirted the island to the south and moved inland from such harbors as Plymouth and Portsmouth—a third mixed group, called Jutes, were too few to count much in the eventual form of the language. The main bodies met along a line running roughly from London to Leeds and Liverpool, and most English dialects today can be in part classified by whether or not they derive from the Anglians to the north and east—their dialect rendered more distinctive by the Danish and Norwegian invaders who later settled there—and contrasting dialects of the Saxons to the south and west. There are, of course, minor dialect areas within these larger groupings.

When Englishmen voyaged to the New World, willy-nilly they took their dialects with them. The Puritans, landing at Plymouth Rock, brought people from East Anglia, north of London. The colony at

Jamestown included many people from the vicinity of London. Thus, very early, and continuingly, dialects from southern and eastern England moved into New England and the southern American colonies. Conversely, when Lord Baltimore brought his Catholics to Maryland and William Penn brought his Quakers to Pennsylvania, they attracted at least some immigrants from farther north and west. All this makes the sorting of speech into the New World sound too simple, but the basic patterns are there; broadly speaking, the dialects that built up on the east coast of what were then the English colonies reflect the dialectal origins of immigrants to the New World. These immigrants in turn brought with them the various sorts of language that certain Germanic groups had acquired as their own varieties of IE speech. Thus when a body of Anglian farmers took their spears, their wives, and their cattle and went west to an offshore island seeking a warmer climate and better pasture, they did not know that they were initiating a dialectal growth that would spread to Seattle, Brisbane, and New Delhi.

THE COURT AND THE COLONIES

Notably, new emigrants were not of the Court, and here we may observe another of the watersheds in the growth of English speech. The Puritan revolution in England had been both economic and religious, but insofar as it was religious it was still economic. The Puritans included a sprinkling of intellectuals like Milton and many common folk like Bunyan, but Royalists commanded the wealth and power. When the royal Court came back from the Continent in 1660 it dominated English life as it never had before, consolidating the landed gentry, the established church, the universities, the growing forces of money and business. This group was tight enough to develop its own social dialect; Court speech became the fashionable speech, taught in the schools, preached from the pulpits, printed in the growing press, and imitated everywhere. It fathered British Received Standard, the norm of prestige usage in the British Isles.

It was not much exported. On the whole, successful people do not become emigrants; they stay and enjoy their comfort and their safety. The impoverished go; the unlucky go; the downtrodden go; the persecuted go. In England if they could get themselves sent to a penal colony the criminals went. The utterly destitute did not go, unless they could sell themselves as indentured servants or could commit a crime venial enough to avoid hanging but bad enough to warrant deportation. They had neither the heart nor the means for a venture like that offered by the New World. They suffered malnutrition, but they stayed. Most of those who went were lower middle class—farm laborers forced off the land, modestly skilled artisans sick of it all, small traders not doing well, and the like. Emphatically they were not of the Court, the landed gentry, the financiers, the prosperous professional people. There was an occasional seeker after religious freedom who happened also to be well to do; there were philanthropists founding utopias in what they hoped would be a better world, but they were few, and they tended not to stay long. Those who survived the rigors of pioneering did not bandy the fashionable new speech of the Court. They talked the dialects, regional and social, of plowmen, tinkers, and London shopmen, even of thieves and prostitutes.

Thus it has been said that modern American English resembles Elizabethan English more than it does modern British English, and within limits this is true. American English descends from the speech of Falstaff's tavern brawlers, not from Prince Hal or Lady Macbeth; from the "rude mechanicals," not from the gentry or even the Malvolios and Sir Tobys, who would be Court hangers-on, or hangers-on of hangers-on. And this shift in British speech habits determined much of what American English was to become. By the end of the eighteenth century the basic American dialects were built up on the east coast and starting to move west—and once a dialect is established it resists change, even changes as powerful as those provided by the horde of nineteenth-century immigrants to the New World. By that time, also, the new Court speech had grown to provide the dominant pattern in the mother country. American dialects reflect the fact that immigrants came from certain parts of the country and in separate waves—the Scottish immigration grew with the depression encouraged by the French wars, the Irish immigration followed the potato famines. They reflect also the fact that lower middle-class folk came, and that after the Court dialect became established, American connections with Britain were mainly limited to the port cities, to Boston, Philadelphia, New York, Baltimore, Charleston, and the like.

One might notice that this British Court speech differed sharply from many of the British dialects carried abroad by emigrants. Many British dialects have a strong /r/—some Northern speech, including some lowland Scots, even preserved the trilled /r/ of Old English. Such /r/ sounds were transmitted to Midland American speech, but not to either Northern or Southern dialects. British low mid and back vowels show great range in the various regional dialects, from /a/ back to /ɔ/. But British Received Standard has tended to restrict /æ/—common in Elizabethan pronunciation—and to develop /ɑ/ and /ɔ/. These pronunciations were characteristic of some New England dialects and were reimported as prestige speech to Boston; meanwhile, most American dialects, including both Midland and Southern speech rely more on /æ/. The same sorts of differences permeate other bodies of colonial English. New Zealand, with a strong aristocratic tradition, has been extensively influenced by Received Standard; more of it appears in Canada than in the United States, because Tories in the United States moved to Canada and Canadians maintained close connections with England. The influence of Received Pronunciation was low in Australia, which was long a penal colony.

Curiously, a very similar development distinguishes New World Spanish dialects from those in the Iberian Peninsula. The Moors overran Spain and remained for roughly a thousand years. Eventually they were driven out by northerners, led by Castilians. When the New World opened up, the emigrants to New Spain came mainly from the southern Spanish areas, notably from Andalusia, and thus Southern dialects have become the basis of most American Spanish speech. Meanwhile, the Court, centered in Toledo and later Madrid, used Castilian, which became the *Español correcto,* recognized as the best Spanish. It has remained in Spain, as Received Standard is in England, a minor dialect as far as number of speakers is concerned, but the approved standard, taught in the schools both in Spain and abroad where Spanish is a second language. Meanwhile, Latin America speaks either mainly Portuguese or non-Castilian Spanish.

Differences abound. For example, Latin *civitates,* city, became Spanish *ciudad.* The Latin /k/, which was probably /s/ in the dominant Latin dialects in Spain, remained /s/ in most dialects, but was changed to another fricative in Castilian /θ/. The Latin /t/ in some positions became the corresponding voiced fricative in Castilian /ð/. Thus the name for *city* in *Español correcto* is /θijoðɑð/, whereas most Spanish speakers, including practically all Latin American speakers, say something closer to /sijədɑd/. Court speech in both England and Spain has become the approved speech, but that happened too late to become universal in the motherland or in much of the New World.

Speech follows language patterns everywhere, and in the New World the principles of dialect continued. The immigrants brought ancestral speech and they continued to grow new dialects, although within limits. Dialects require time and some uniformity, and in the newer English-speaking areas history is young and the population fluid. Thus you may notice more change going from one parish to the next in England than from one state to the next in the Middle West, and Australia and Canada show even less diversity. One sort of growth has been notable in the New World, however—the speech of the Blacks.

In part Black English reflects merely the universal working of dialect. Inevitably, Black speech differs in Harlem, the Chicago South Side, and Watts, California. Africans were brought here; most of them were ignorant of European culture, including European languages. They learned English through the generations, some of it from overseers in the fields, some from maids in the kitchen, some from one another. Inevitably, they developed dialects. When they moved north and west, they carried these dialects with them. Harlem, much the oldest large Negro settlement, contains more mulattos and quadroons than do the others, more descendants of escaped slaves from Virginia and the other border states. Chicago received Blacks from the New Orleans delta, from Kentucky and Tennessee; Blacks went west to Watts from Texas. All this is to be expected. The Blacks brought a few words that have become standard American—*goober* for peanut, possibly *buckaroo* for white man, from *buckra* (although that may have come through Mexican *vaquero*, cowboy), and probably *tote,* and many that have had local currency. This sort of thing happened variously to all immigrants, and the Negro was in effect an involuntary immigrant.

PIDGINS AND THEIR OFFSPRING

But there is also something irregular about Black speech. Immigrants usually lose their language in a few generations. Pennsylvania Dutch has survived, but it is being eroded, and its speakers were a closely knit group, whereas Black English persists after more than three centuries. Black speech characteristics are not due to anything physical; language is mainly social, and black idioms do not reflect the influence of thick lips or short noses. A black child brought up in a white family in a white community will speak like his companions. Part of this persistence of Black English reflects the life of many Blacks in slave quarters, and after emancipation, social segregation. More recently Blacks have lived in urban ghettos. But most Blacks, whether they now work on Detroit assembly lines or are janitors in Minneapolis apartment houses, use tones of voice, stresses, even grammar that they could not have learned from whites. White speakers do not have them, and never have had them. Furthermore, this Black English is not just standard English spoken clumsily; a Black speaker may use *be, been,* and *done* as verbal auxiliaries in ways foreign to white speakers, but their use is not inept or irregular. Research has recently revealed that Negro verbs follow strict rules; *he don go* and *he don be goin* are correct verbs although different verbs in Black English, whereas *he don goin* would be incorrect, and would in effect never be heard. That is, Black English can probably not be called a language, but it works somewhat like one.

Lately we have had a bizarre explanation for all this, a theory not accepted by all students of language, but intriguing, and it must have some truth. This thesis for the origin of Black English takes account of the maritime movement into Northwest Africa in the sixteenth century and after. The Portuguese came first—that may be the way we get *pickaninny* from Portuguese—then the French and English. These traders and the natives devised a *pidgin,* that is, a limited sort of speech, using bits out of two or more languages, with enough of all of them so that communication is possible. Because the native speakers of this lingua franca use it most, it is likely to utilize local grammar, including local pitch patterns; because objects of trade are likely to be those either bought or brought by the traders, nouns may be those of the distant language, in this case Portuguese, French, or English.

During the decades such pidgins must have been built up along the West African coast, including at least some using English and some from such places as Sierra Leone, from whence came so many American slaves. Natives captured by slavers, or sold into slavery by their rulers, would have included many of them. And when these Blacks were transported, those who knew nothing but a local African speech would learn this pidgin from their fellow slaves—that was, in effect, the only way many of them could learn, because, living in slave quarters, they had little chance to do anything but take orders, and even the slave driver talked pidgin, which he had learned from slaves who knew it. Thus out of West African pidgin may have come Plantation Creole, which coalesced with the speech brought by immigrants from England to form the subsequent white Southern dialects. According to this thesis, bizarre Southern speech such as Goose Creek Gulla and related coastal accents roughly preserve Plantation Creole as it was spoken a couple of centuries ago. (Just to keep our terms straight, we might notice that when two or more languages blend so that each loses its character we say they have been creolized. Presumably, Plantation Creole resulted from a jumbling of Southern American English, West African Pidgin, and various West African tongues.)

Nor is this all. Believers in the West African Pidgin suggest that it was carried not only to the English colonies in America, but to the West Indies, where it thrives in various versions. It moved east, also, going to the East Indies. Thus pidgin was scattered around the world; it was the way a Black man talked if he had to talk to a white man. It picked up some Chinese and became Chinese pidgin. It was taught to American Indians by runaway slaves that found harbor with them—this collaboration of Indians and escaped Blacks against their common enemy is well-attested for the Seminoles, although less for most tribes. Thus, if one accepts this thesis, when a Chinese cook, working for a railroad gang on an early California railroad, married an Indian woman, they might find they could converse a bit. The two pidgins they spoke had met after having circled the globe, going both east and west from the West African pidgin center.

THE PROBLEM OF BLACK ENGLISH

So now Black English is a problem. Through the centuries, the speech of Negroes had much more to do with the present course of Southern American speech than the defenders of segregation and white supremacy like to admit, but this triumph has not solved the personal problems of many Black speakers. For generations Black dialects throve. On the plantations, black faces outnumbered white faces, and in language, numbers count. Furthermore, white babies were given to Black mammies to care for, even to nurse, and as we have seen—although proud Southern belles did not understand this—much of a person's language, whoever he is, is learned in infancy and by imitation of whatever he hears. And then there was the playground; black and white children played together, and language is learned more on the playground than anywhere else, more than in the schoolroom or the home. More pickaninnies came from the slave quarters than there were little ladies and gentlemen from the "big house." Thus the southern Negroes powerfully affected southern speech, but they never thoroughly taught their masters the West African grammar and pitch patterns that their ancestors had brought. And they never entirely lost this heritage themselves. They bequeathed problems to their children.

Now Blacks find their racial pride and their personal well-being at odds. Very rightly they view their language as part of them, not to be demeaned—a linguist would go farther, and say that all dialects are equal, that Black speech is as good as any other. If it is not as fashionable as Back Bay Bostonese, it preserves what the fashionable dialects never had and would have been lost except for so-called dialect speakers. Yet it is not standard speech, and being "underprivileged" results more from not commanding standard speech than from any other one thing. And the more complex and technical American society becomes, the more it relies on elaborate education, the more the nonstandard speaker suffers.

So what can be done about the ghettos? Ghettos offer few futures, and the more ghetto-bound the child becomes, the worse his chances. Whether he owes his dialect to the Southern slave driver or the West African pidgin, the fact is that his speech handicaps him. One solution that shows some promise is to teach the ghetto child standard English as he would be taught if he had been born to Arabic or Chinese, to teach him a new dialect as though it were a new language. No effort is made to root out his native speech. He keeps it and uses it when he wants to, but he is also taught something approaching standard English, which he can use when he needs it, and he is drilled in this so assiduously that he becomes in effect bilingual—though *diglossic* or *bidialectal* are approved terms when a speaker uses two dialects for different audiences. This is, of course, what some Blacks did spontaneously during slavery days. European visitors would comment on the Black houseservant who spoke English indistinguishable from that of the family, but the same person, back in the slave quarters, would talk the pidgin that was a lingua franca of Black slavery.

So languages continue to live by dialects. As travel and communication increase, as education becomes more nearly universal, as social differences are leveled, the importance of dialect declines. Except for the special problem of the Blacks, the Indians, the Puerto Ricans, and the Chicanos, dialects in America are less important than in Britain. Languages are always tending to draw together at the same time they pull apart; the day may come when the forces of coherence triumph in English. But that day is not yet, if ever. For a long time the deep-seated urge to grow language diversity will work throughout English and all other languages.

11

LANGUAGE
AS FASHION

USAGE

According to apparently reliable testimony, there was once a grave-stone in Wales bearing the following inscription:

> Let
> Farts go free
> Wherever you be
> For the stoppage of one
> Was the killing of me

This is palpably crude poetry and probably faulty diagnostics. One doubts that any single instance of restrained flatulence was fatal, so that the inscription has little to tell us except that linguistic manners have changed. Here a word that in subsequent generations was never heard in polite society is paraded in the most solemn circumstances.

Other evidence bears similar witness. One of the loveliest lyrics in the language, the justly admired "Sumer is Icumen In," contains the following line:

Bulluc sterteth, buck verteth.

The first two words mean that an ox leaped, and the last two may mean that a buck sheep dodged about, *verteth* being taken as related to our word *veer*. But that is improbable; the poem dates about 1240, a good two centuries before the first known appearance of *veer* in English. More likely *verteth* is the same word for that action approved in headstone doggerel as salubrious. To identify the common if naughty word one has only to remove the ending *-eth,* recognize that *e* and *a* are common alternate spellings in Middle English, and that in some dialects initial fricatives were voiced so that /f/ appears as /v/, as in *fox* and *vixen*. With these changes *verteth* becomes the familiar four-letter word—no doubt the improbable etymology from Latin *vibrare* was a comfort to school teachers who, in more Victorian days than ours, had to read the poem aloud in class. In the Middle Ages, apparently, what has more delicately been called breaking wind was one of the welcome bucolic sounds of spring, and the versifier used a homey Old English word for it.

If the occurrence of the word in "Sumer is Icumen In" is uncertain, others are not. In his *Friar's Tale* Chaucer introduces an ingenious device by which the results of flatulence can be divided equally among twelve monks, each greedy for a share in a supposed bequest. Chaucer does not hesitate to use the vigorous four-letter word repeatedly, and a scribe repeated it in a heading. Nor, apparently, did the auditors do anything but laugh, although on another occasion the possible impropriety of another tale was discussed, and many medieval persons felt that swearing by God's bones was in questionable taste. One should remember, also, that the Chaucer tale accompanied a pious journey to the shrine of a saint and that the audience numbered several ecclesiastics, including the tale-teller, the devout Parson, and a prioress doing her best to act like a great lady, along with very respectable laymen and even the Knight, who, we are informed, never used any *villany* (bad language) at all. Nor were the witty Greeks bothered by their form of the word. Recalling that /f/ in English is likely to appear as /p/ in Greek, we can plausibly guess that the *partridge* gets its name from the startling sound of beating wings as the bird roars away.

Obviously, fashions in language change and just recently people in

English-speaking countries have witnessed a swing toward latitudinar-
ianism—some would say laxity—in terms concerning copulation, uri-
nation, and defecation. A century or so ago one could discuss such matters only if he used terms sufficiently Latinate and medical, as I have
just done. More recently, familiar words for earthy actions could be
used with restraint, in scholarly journals or other places where children
and laymen, particularly ladies, would not be likely to see them. Now
any word can pass unmentioned and almost unnoticed in novels and
on the stage, although not yet on television or in most newspapers. But
even broadcast English has been so liberalized that nonpious references
to the deity are not much inhibited, although only a few years ago
locutions like "God damn it!" and "Go to hell" were never heard on
the air. And it will be apparent that even today I have endeavored to
forfend my publisher by using naughty words only when I can quote
them from an innocent old gravestone, or can enshroud them in Middle
English.

TABOO IN LANGUAGE

All this involves what is called *taboo,* from a Polynesian word for
objects unmentionable for religious or other reasons. All peoples have
taboos, more or less numerous, more or less rigidly observed, more or
less transient. The transliteration *Jehovah* stems from avoiding the
name of the Hebrew deity; many tribes forbid a man to use the name
of his mother-in-law; a Plains Indian woman had to avoid seeing or
speaking to anyone while she was menstruating. Such taboos vary from
culture to culture, even from time to time. According to an apparently
reliable account, soon after the turn of the century the editor of an
American magazine for women was delighted to buy the first run of a
story by a popular British novelist, but was horrified to find that the
hero in the yarn tossed off a glass of wine. The editor cabled the author,
identifying the passage, and saying *"Ladies' Home Journal* policy for-
bids reference to alcoholic beverages; please advise." The author,
amused and possibly irked, wired back, "Make it Mellon's Food."
Mellon's Food was a pablum for babies, and the editor had perforce
to print the wicked four-letter word *wine.* With the years the policy
has changed; it has gone the way of all taboos, sooner or later, but however illogical, unreasonable, or unfounded they may seem after the

reason for them is forgotten and before their practice has been abandoned, taboos are powerful in society and hence in language, at least for a time and usually for a long time.

Part of the problem with usage arises from fashion in language being more than one thing. As we have just seen, some locutions become taboo; in English they may be called vulgar. And as we have noticed in an earlier chapter, terms that arise from having fun with language may be called slang, and disapproved by those who do not use it, particularly by those who do not understand it and would mostly be incapable of inventing it.

Some language is disapproved because it suggests ignorance or a lowly origin; it is often called *bad grammar,* although questions of grammar strictly understood are usually not involved: "He clumb the tree" and "It hain't fittin fer nothin" are not bad grammar in the sense that they are incomprehensible to a native or that any of the words is syntactically out of place. But no well-bred or well-educated speaker of English would be likely to use such sentences, and they are deprecated because they suggest crudity, not because they flout the grammatical patterns of the language. Many Englishmen were long contemptuous of American speech because, New World dialects having sprung from the speech of servants and lower middle-class folk, the language of even an educated American sounded in England like the language of yokels and the generally ill-bred.

HOW GOOD GRAMMAR GOES BAD

Much so-called "bad grammar" is only old grammar, once fashionable but now out of favor. Most speakers who pride themselves on their language and feel that they are living examples of what language should be do not like language change. They want to speak the language as it has been spoken, and they believe they do. Of course devotion to antiquity for antiquity's sake is nonsense; not the most tunnel-visioned purist speaks Proto-Indo-European, but conservatism has its place in language. If careful speakers of the language did not try to preserve it, it probably could not maintain the currency necessary for survival. But all languages change all the time, and are no worse off for doing so, although many changes, normal and healthy in themselves, have been the father of what is popularly known as "bad grammar."

Consider the English verb. As we have seen, PIE verbs embodied much that concerned time, and this evidence of time was revealed by what is called *ablaut,* a change of sound within the verb form. A few modern verbs have preserved some of this ablaut; *write, wrote, written; sing, sang, sung; buy, bought; teach, taught; find, found; begin, began, begun; choose, chose, chosen*—some fifty of them. As one would expect, because language is orderly within limits, PIE speakers had ways of making such verbs. Starting with a stem, which might have been any of several vowels or consonants, they could add one qualitative ablaut and one quantitative one. These ablauts affected *e* or *o,* long or short, or they could both be absent in what is called zero-grade. For example, PIE had a word *ridan;* to this could be added an *e*-ablaut and an *o*-ablaut, producing *ridan, rad, ridon, ridden* as principal parts in Old English, our *ride, rode, ridden.*

Then something happened to IE speakers. Many started using more analytic devices and fewer synthetic ones; that is, they relied more on the order of words and the grammatical force of individual words like prepositions, and less on change in the shape of words. And of all the IE languages, English moved fastest and farthest toward analysis. Thus for centuries no English verbs have been devised by using the *ride-rode-ridden* pattern. Instead, phrasal verbs were developed like *I am going to ride, I have been riding,* and insofar as any inflectional change was needed, /d/ was added to the past and the past participle. This consonant, which might be preceded by a vowel for convenience to make /əd/ or could be changed to the corresponding voiceless consonant /t/, produced variants like *spoiled* and *spoilt.* Something similar characterizes many other IE languages.

Now we should recall that the millennia when English was undergoing its great growth were the times after ablaut verbs were being made. The Germanic peoples encountered the sea, and needed new words, including verbs. They dealt with Roman traders, who used an ablaut system but a different one; when words were borrowed from Latin they were made into verbs with the new endings. If a convert turned to *Christ* he was *christened.* Then the great flood of loan words came; if they were verbs they were treated like English verbs, and if they were nouns and a verb form was needed, the new term fell into the pattern that was by now conventional in English. Our word *orbit* comes from a Latin word meaning *wheel;* needing forms for a word *to orbit* any child would know how to make them. He would say *orbited,* not *erbit, arbit,* or *urbit.*

At length the new practice with verbs—after the manner of habits and principles—became inclusive. Verbs that had once indicated tense with the old ablaut system were changed to the new one; the verb *hladan, hlod, hlodon, hladen* became our word *load, loaded; giellan, geal, gullon, gollon* became our *yield, yielded.* Some verbs having the old forms just vanished; some words always do vanish, but perhaps those that seemed now to have irregular or old-fashioned forms vanished the more easily for that. Words like *belgan,* to be angry, and *helan,* to conceal, do not exist any more; most of these words have been replaced by Romance words like *conceal* but some have not been. We have no single verb meaning *to be angry,* and have had to concoct a phrasal verb to express the idea.

This shift in verb systems aggravated usage problems. Most ablaut verbs withered away or were replaced by the new-fashioned shape. Some survived without much loss, as we have seen; others survived with special uses. *Meltan* was regularized to *melt, melted,* but we can still use the old past participle in *molten* metal; *drencan* survived as *drink, drank, drunk,* and in some dialects one can say "He had drunken his draft," but in most dialects *drunken* can be used only as a modifier. Thus some of these old forms have preserved their respectability, albeit with limited use, but most did not fare so well.

Consider *climb.* It comes from Old English *climban,* and like most Old English verbs that survived, it was normalized to *climb, climbed.* But *climbed* is not a fancy word like *ascend,* which in part superseded it. It was used by ordinary people, and old forms like *klim, klom, kloom,* and *klum* survived also, although they were mostly branded as *Dial.* or "bad grammar." Or consider *to eat.* It came from *ettan, aet, eton, etten* and has been standardized to *eat, ate, eaten.* Other forms like *ett, itt, aet, eated, etted,* and *eat* as a preterite are quite as justifiable, but they are now out of fashion and hence not good usage.

One of the worst jumbles, of course, involves *to be.* As we have seen, it comes from three old verbs, and a few forms have been standardized, but we might just as well have called some other forms "right," or "correct," such as *ain't, hain't, am't, is'n, beeun, wesen, nosent, bane,* and dozens of others—some, of course, have survived dialectally. There is great variety even among accepted terms; for *been* Received Standard has /bijn/, rhyming with *seen,* whereas most American and some British dialects have /bin/, and the state of *be* is uncertain as an imperative or conditional. Futhermore, in the development of phrasal verbs, several terms were tried as auxiliaries—including *fare, let,* and a lost verb related to *worth*—most of them now abandoned. Forms of *do* are now standardized in *did* and *done,* although variants survive in Black English. Thus much so-called bad grammar only preserves forms now out of fashion; historically the unfashionable shapes are as good as the fashionable ones, sometimes better. *Went* is no better logically and traditionally than *bin gone* and *am went,* but one has survived in the prestige dialects and the others have not. And of course fashionable terms are not "right" in any real sense; language is logical and traditional within limits, but in the end language use will triumph. Whatever is used, especially in the fashionable dialects, will become good usage and whatever is not established in such dialects will be poor usage, or even "bad grammar." That, whether we like it or not, is the way society and language work.

BORROWING AND USAGE

A continuing source of usage problems stems from borrowing. As we have seen, borrowed locutions are always altered, usually in several ways. Thus, at a minimum, two forms for a borrowed word or phrase are likely to be vying for the stability of being "correct," one an approximation of the locution before borrowing, preserved by those who have some acquaintance with the original tongue, and another that approaches the patterns of the borrowing language, in this instance English. For example, *agenda* comes from Latin, being made from a word meaning *do,* plus a sign of the present participle. Thus it means *things to be done.* It is a plural, with a singular *agendum,* one thing to be done. But *agenda* ends in *a,* and thus in English seems to be a singular; accordingly, a new plural has developed, *agendas,* deplored by all users of Latin, but surely to become standard, sooner or later. Similarly, scientists and scholars speak of *these data,* but many people say *this data* or *these datas,* and eventually, no doubt, everybody will. Similarly, *cactus,* a Latin singular, has kept its Latin plural, *cacti,* but because that does not sound like an English plural, *cactuses* has developed, and some people wonder which is right. Nobody uses *circi* any more as a plural of *circus*.

This sort of thing leads inevitably to confusion in usage. An Arabic word for a supernatural being that can take human form can be transliterated *jinni, ginii, djineeya, genie, jinee, gini, ginnee, djin, djinnee,* and in dozens of other ways. Which way is "correct"? Only usage can decide, if it ever does, and the decision, when it comes, will not be based on any obvious, incontrovertible, logical decision. And with American concern for Arabian oil, Japanese industry, Russian political maneuvers, and Chinese populations—all involving languages from which transliterations are confounding—confusion in American usage will continue, and in some ways grow worse.

Thus usage is fostered by tradition and rooted in emotion. People get furious about it, and usually know little of it. It promotes wrath in the righteous and humility in the humble. But like the poor, we have it always with us, for it, too, is rooted in the nature of cantankerous, egocentric man.

USAGE AND WHAT TO DO ABOUT IT

If usage is a natural problem, it is still a problem, a very real one. Nonstandard diction can harm its users, and most cultured persons know this. Parents, especially, may be sensitive to it. And rightly. But what can one do about usage? What should one do about it? And—at least as important—what should one *not* do about it?

For remedial purposes, usage presents two kinds of problems with different sorts of answers, one sort for adults, one for youngsters. Almost never can a person who has grown to maturity using an unfashionable dialect eradicate it or substitute another dialect for it. Change is too hard for adults, and the usages to be learned too numerous. Something can be done; any intelligent adult can alter some usages if he wants to work hard enough. He should select only those usages that are most important for him, inform himself copiously about them, and practice standard use assiduously. All good dictionaries give some help with usage, although those that make a to-do about usage panels and percentages may seem more authoritative than they are, and some are so reactionary that they have little practical use. On the whole the dictionaries of usage serve best, their editors having enough space to provide details. Personally, I like Margaret M. Bryant, *Current American Usage* (New York: Funk and Wagnalls, 1962, and Bergen Evans and Cornelia Evans, *A Dictionary of Contemporary American Usage* (New York: Random House, 1957). They are scholarly, relatively objective, and sensible. The old standard for British idiom, H. W. Fowler, *A Dictionary of Modern English Usage,* is out of date but has been capably revised by Sir Ernest Gowers, 2nd ed. (New York and Oxford: Oxford University Press, 1965).

A word of caution may be in order. Nobody, not even a devoted adult, should try too hard to correct his usage. After all, language has more important aspects than current fashion. Vigor, clarity, charm, and copiousness of speech are much more important. Many a man who says *ain't* and *he don't* has risen to high office or has accumulated a fortune, has married a lovely wife and made many friends, who soon learned to ignore his nonstandard speech. And if one tries too hard to be "correct" he may succeed only in being prissy. He could better invest his efforts in learning to use the language well.

With youngsters the cure is quite different. They can learn quantities of new usage if they want to, but they have to want to. They may even learn to distinguish *imply* and *infer, lie* and *lay.* A teacher can help them; so can their parents, but usage is so complex that nobody can teach them much of it. They have to learn it voluntarily, and—to be very successful—eagerly. Thus adults can help them most, if at all, by providing incentives to learn, along with hard information as to what is standard and what is not, and by not hindering (see Chapter 9). The worst thing an adult can do in language is to try to beat good usage into a child, with either physical or moral suasion. At best, parental nagging is likely to develop passive resistance that would put a Gandhi to shame. At worst, the parent is likely to stimulate a sort of juvenile guerilla warfare, with the child getting his revenge learning the most derogated usages he can acquire. Or he may be stunted mentally by his fear of language and its self-appointed policers.

Much good can be done in the cultivation of approved usage, but perhaps nowhere else in speech can so much harm be done with such good intentions.

12

LANGUAGE,
THE MOTHER OF TOOLS

Civilized and barbaric peoples differ in this: one has developed or has borrowed tools to enlarge language; the other has not. The distinction is obvious, but it is also causative; language helped make mankind human, but extensions of language that made it able to work through time and space helped man become civilized. Such tools are late; man had to become somewhat tamed before he could develop them, but once language could last beyond the moment of breath, beyond the space in which a listener could hear a speaker, civilization speeded up. Now it accelerates astronomically, and means to enlarge language grow with it.

The basic tool, although not the only one, was writing. It started with pictures, perhaps pictures like those in European caves portraying game animals, probably intended to promote magical power in the hunt. The designs may have resembled those pecked by American Indians into rocks; the doings of stick men, the placation of deities, maybe just doodling. Such pictures became signs, even symbols, and systems of symbols.

We know of three mainstreams of writing, which may have had a common ancestor, from cultures centered on great rivers. In China, along the Yang-tze-Kiang and Huang Ho Rivers, pictures became symbols for objects and stylizations of the pictured words for these objects. Terms were combined, often figuratively; the east was the sun seen through trees, a wife was a woman in a house. But Chinese writing remained limited to representations of words, to *logograms*—Greek *logos* meaning word, plus *-gram*, something written—also called *ideograms*, representations of ideas. In southwestern Asia, especially along the Tigris-Euphrates River valleys, well before 3000 B.C., the Sumers were using a syllabary. In this writing system, a symbol developed from a picture so that it could be used for a syllable, a consonant sound plus a vowel. That is, the writing included both sound and meaning in one system, although it was a bit cumbersome because any language will have many combinations of sound.

BIRTH OF THE ALPHABET

The third system developed at the eastern end of the Mediterranean, apparently stemming from the Egyptians along the Nile. They developed ideographic writing, and whether or not they got the idea from the Hittites and Akkads who had followed the Sumers, they used a syllabary along with their ideograms, and some of the syllables were one sound only. That is, a symbol had now become the representation of one sound, and once such sounds could be organized into a system an alphabet was possible. No alphabet was organized, however, until the ingenious Greeks got hold of the idea, probably through Semites, notably the Phoenicians.

The alphabet worked by a combination of rebuses, puns, and acronymics. For example, take the word *belief*. In a rebus we could represent *be-* as a honey bee, and *-lief* as a *leaf*. We could then take the first sound in each of these words to make an acronym, BL, and these representations of /b/ and /l/ could be used to spell the word or to appear with other such symbols in any combination to represent sequences of sounds and their corresponding uses and meanings.

Need and accident altered the Semitic symbols. One, called *aleph* for an ox, became Greek *alpha* and our *a;* the symbol was made of a line with two branching intersecting lines, presumably representing the head and horns of an ox. It was turned on the side and reversed—this was easy in Greek, which was written either left to right or right to left, or alternately left and right. Likewise, our letter *B* comes from *beth,* meaning house, which became Greek *beta,* with the representation of a house obscured through the centuries. Similarly, *gimmel* for *camel* became Greek *gamma,* providing us with both *C* and *G.* And so on through the list; *Z* came from a word for *weapon,* perhaps because, looking about like a modern capital *I,* the Semitic *Z* suggested a spear or dagger. Thus an ancient writing system became an alphabetic system, which was so obviously the best sort of writing medium that the method spread—particularly because it was taken up by the Indo-European peoples. They carried the Latin alphabet all over the world.

Our alphabet is the best one ever developed because it is the only one. We are lucky to be born to it; it took thousands of years and a curious concatenation of peoples, but it is in many ways inadequate because it bears within it the scars of its growth. Even its birthmarks disfigure it. Semitic languages have few vowels; thus Semitic syllabaries tended to be signs for consonants plus a flick—it is the ancestor of our apostrophe—which marked the place where a vowel was present but unwritten, any vowel. We can approximate the device by spelling Kalamazoo as K'L'M'Z'; the system was compact and served well enough for a language having few vowels, and used mainly by specialists for limited purposes.

THE BREAKDOWN OF THE ALPHABET

But the Semitic consonantal system was inadequate for Indo-European languages, which have numerous vowel sounds. The Greeks adapted the alphabet—somewhat. *Aleph* had formerly begun with a consonant, lost by the time the symbol was borrowed; to the Greeks it seemed to begin with a vowel, and they used it for *alpha,* our *a.* Similarly, they got the ancestors for our *o* and *e* by utilizing other unneeded signs for consonants—*omega* was *o-mega,* that is *o-big,* and our *E* came from a Semitic symbol that looked rather like a rake turned sideways, used for HE, which lost its aspiration and seemed to the Greeks to be a vowel. It was epsilon, of which our shape *e* dervies from the script sign. *Yod,* a consonant, was split into variant forms, which gave us *j* and *i*—one more vowel. Likewise, *V* was a good form to carve into wood or stone, but a rounded form was handier for script; *V* split into *V* and *U*—one more vowel. Thus the Romans inherited five signs for vowels where once there had been none—*a, e, i, o,* and *u*—but modern English needs at least ten signs if our common vowel sounds are to be directly represented—fifteen would be better. Accordingly, we have this curious result: modern IE languages have a relatively stable body of consonants, partly because consonant sounds tend to be fixed in the mouth at points like the lips and teeth, and partly because they descend from an adequate system of symbols in the Semitic languages. On the other hand, our vowels and the symbols for them are much disturbed, partly because vowels shift readily anyhow and tend to develop glides and combine into diphthongs, but partly because we have never had an adequate sequence of signs for vowels, only those that the Greeks developed. These last existed at all only because the Greeks were both ingenious and ignorant—they did not know what some of the signs they borrowed were good for. And nobody asked what vowel signs were needed and then devised a sufficient body of signs. Or if he did, he was ignored. Aristotle might have made such an appraisal, but if he did his fellow Athenians did not utilize the suggestion. That is the difficulty with an alphabet; it is no good unless people will use it; and if a brilliant Greek suggested a sensible alphabet he would not have been the first—or the last—of the intelligentsia to find himself ignored or ridiculed by his fellowmen for having made a good proposal.

Changes continued but they were sporadic and the vowel problem for IE languages was never adequately dealt with. For some of the Slavic languages, one St. Cyril helped a bit; in adapting the Greek alphabet to Church Slavonic—and hence to Russian—he added signs where he thought they were needed, and thus Russian has nothing like the dearth of English vowels. One could wish that more Western saints had been interested in language, even at the expense of a few dragons unslain and a few sparrows unfed. Diacritical marks have helped; French distinguishes *e*-sounds with accents, German uses umlauts, the Scandinavian languages have incorporated several devices, but diacritical markings are clumsy at best, and on the whole the vowel signs remain what they became in Classical times.

The Romans ordered the alphabet somewhat, and were responsible for its first great spread through the use of Latin as an international learned and diplomatic medium. There were other minor changes. *U* doubled became double-*u*, written *w*, the ligatured form of two *v*'s—more accurately called double-*v* in German—and was introduced into England by Norman scribes to replace an Anglo-Saxon letter strange to them, a Runic sign called *wenn*. Two other Runic signs, þ and ð, introduced into Old English for sounds not in Latin, were replaced by *th,* and other linkages like *gh, ch,* and *sh* were devised for sounds not in Latin or French. The letter *i* was slightly altered; it was written as a straight vertical line, and was readily confused. In a widespread continental script *m* was written with three strokes, *n* and *u* with two. Spaces between letters were often not very prominent. Thus *minimum,* if the word had existed, could have been written with fifteen vertical lines. Even a word like *mine* could be confusing; spelled without *e* it was six lines. Accordingly, scribes marked with a flick the vertical line meant to be a vowel, and in printing the flick became the dot over the *i.* Such minor revisions helped, but they were not enough, especially as language use grew. An inscription system adequate to mark graves, to preserve religious texts, and to promulgate laws sufficed for early uses of writing, but as language became the medium of long communications that had to be read easily and rapidly by all sorts of people, the ancient media became less and less adequate.

AND NOW, SPELLING

Accordingly, the system of inscription was bolstered with what we call spelling. If the original alphabet had been good enough it would not have needed crutches like subsidiary systems, but even the Greeks found they needed spelling conventions, and the Romans needed them even more. As Latin spread, so did confusion. English provides a good case.

Early Old English, of course, was not a written language; the Germanic peoples did not know how to write. Culture came north with priests who used Latin; when they had to write the vernacular, they used Latin symbols. The transfer presented problems, but the priests were professionals writing for other professionals, and they managed. For simplicity, I shall ignore them.

In Middle English, troubles were various, not to say vexing. Scribes endeavored to use letters as symbols for sound, but there was no consistency in the sounds. Several dialects had grown from the Saxon speech of the southwest, which for a time after Alfred had become a sort of Court speech. The descendant of Jutish persisted in the southeast, where Canterbury became a center of learning. Anglian accents had proliferated in central and eastern England, and had become the basis of a new dialect of London. To the north another sort of Anglian, heavily influenced by Scandinavian, merged into other dialects farther north tinged by Celtic. French had moved in very irregularly, heavily in the London and Edinburgh areas, very sparsely to the west. Sounds shifted variously; diphthongs common in Saxon dialects were unknown to Anglian speech, so that our word *world* was *werld* to the east, *weorld* to the west; our *light* could be *leoht* or *liht*. English /ɣ/ and /χ/ dropped out, blended into diphthongs, or became other vowels; thus OE *burh* /buərχ/ became words now spelled as differently as *burg*, *bury*, *-boro*, *burrough*, *-bi*, and *brough* (preserved in place-names). OE /k/ became /č/ and /sk/ became /š/, but not in all dialects, so that we now have *church* from southern England, *kirk* from the north. Likewise to the south, pronunciations like *shoe, shove*, and *shoot* developed whereas Scandinavian, Dutch, and various conservative influences preserved spellings like *scoot, scop*, and *skit*.

Stress confused pronunciation and accordingly spelling. The alphabet had come from Latin, which had length variation with stresses—such as there were—far on in the word. English, on the other hand, had inherited a heavy stress from Germanic, usually on the first syllable not a prefix. Thus stresses in borrowed words were always shifting, changing the qualities of vowels. Furthermore, there were not enough Latin vowel signs to distinguish the stressed from the unstressed vowels of English. So the scribes adopted various devices to provide, in effect, more vowels, but they did not use the same system. Some would double consonants after short or slack vowels, if they thought the reader might not guess that the vowel was short. Others did not, nor did they all guess alike. Some added an extra vowel sign to show that a vowel was stressed; for this purpose *e* was common in the south, and thus we get such spellings as *mete* and *meet*, whereas in the north *i* or *y* served the same purpose, but *i* and *y* served also to indicate glides, as when the /g/ fell out so that *magden* and *saegde* became our *maid* and *said*. And of course this was the time of the Great English Vowel Shift, described earlier, so that many vowels were moving, and at different times and rates in the various dialects.

For assorted reasons, words were shortening. The language was moving from synthetic grammar toward analytic grammar, and as part of this process endings were dropping off or being clipped. *Cneowum* has been cut to our word *knee;* that is, /kneəwum/ became /nij/. *Byrthenna* became *burdens,* and of course an ending in process of weakening could appear as *e* in spelling, probably /i/ or /ə/ in pronunciation. Plurals were in a shambles; Old English had used a half-dozen declensional systems inherited from Germanic, but was losing most of them and standardizing variously. On the whole, Southern dialects used /s/ or /z/ as signs of the plural, northern dialects /n/, but there were others too, so that *childs, childer, childen, childers, childens,* and *childeren* were current (the last three being double plurals).

There was always the possibility of syncopation, words shrinking as a consonant or a whole syllable vanished in the ease of speech. A *lord* and his *lady* had been the *hlaffweard* (guardian of the loaf) and the *hlaffdige* (bread-maker); both consonants and vowels were simplified. Changes were especially notable in loan words with strange sounds, shifts of accent, and the like; Old French *quartrefourks* became *Carfax,* the center of Oxford. Something like *baillage* got cut down to *bail,* and *quinquefolium* became *sincfoil,* now somewhat restored to *cinquefoil.*

Even the letters were confused. Old English scribes had developed traditions as to how Latin signs were to represent English phonemes, and native scribes went on using them, but Norman scribes introduced French ways of writing, and ecclesiastical scribes returned to the Latin tradition, especially for the host of abbreviations used to shorten words with long endings—a line over a letter could mean *m* or *n,* a curlicue after it could stand for *re, er, or, ir,* and the like. The sound /k/, more or less doubled, could be spelled *c, k, qu, h, cc, kk, ck,* and *gh.* Digraphs were developed for sounds the Anglo-Normans did not know how to write, *gh, hg, gg, ch, sh, sch, skh, ssch.*

A few letters were interchangeable; some scribes used *u* and *v* in accordance with the present practice, but some reversed them, and more used one or the other for both purposes. Thus *love* could be spelled *luu, lvv, luv, lvu, lww, lvww, luww,* etc., and because the distinction between /f/ and /v/ was by no means consistent, or the sound /ʊ/ constant, there were spellings like *loff, lvf, lluuf,* and *lvvf.* Some letters were readily confused: *y,* the script form of *þ,* and a Runic sign called *wenn,* used for /w/, were similar in shape. A revived *yod,* written various ways but often like a *z* with a curlicue (ȝ) was common for various uses, pairing with *g, j, h, z, k,* and *þ.* The Runic signs *þ* and *ð,* along with *th* and *ht,* were used for either of the sounds now associated with *th,* /θ/ and /ð/.

For example, consider the feminine singular pronoun, our word *she.*

In Old English it had probably been something like /χej/. The sound /χ/ was changing, and the Normans had no way to spell it; vowels in open syllables tend to be unstable. Accordingly, the word was spelled *he, hi, heo, hie, she, sheo, shio, shee, shei, sche, scheo, schoj, sco, scoj,* etc. This was, of course, a common word known to everyone; spelling was not simplified for rare words, especially for long, borrowed words. Not until printing became common, in the seventeenth century, was there anything approaching uniformity in spelling.

NEXT, PUNCTUATION

The alphabet had other shortcomings as well. It did not even raise the problems inherent in what we have called the suprasegmentals— that is, the patterns of the sentence as revealed through stress, pitch of the voice, pauses, and the like. Scribes started early to use various dots and flicks of the pen, but there was no system and not even much similarity; some scribes did not even separate words with a space, although some apparently tried to use spaces of various lengths, with long ones to mark sentences. When *Beowulf* was discovered it was thought to be prose, because neither a new line nor a capital letter is used to distinguish a verse. By the Middle Ages most of the marks of punctuation we now recognize were used for something, in fact, with various scribes, for almost anything. There were also signs now lost, a semicolon upside down, a period above the line of writing, a colon on its side, and the like. Caxton in some books used a slant line for a maid-of-all-work signal for any pause. As late as the eighteenth century, important nouns were capped, and some writers still use small caps throughout for proper names. Again, the printers were the most important standardizers, and even today there is some uncertainty as to what a comma is good for.

Actually, our writing system is not so clumsy as a catalogue of its horrors may suggest. A system seemingly better might be worse. A good set of letters, with one letter for each sound and only one sound for a letter, would be easy to devise; in effect we have one already in the phonetic alphabet. Punctuation could readily be expanded; the structural linguists have worked out means of recording pitch, stress, tone, and juncture. All these could be combined into a comprehensive set of symbols, and the result would be impractical for most purposes. The fact is that language is so complex that any concatenation of signs extensive enough to describe the production of a speaker would be scientifically revealing but awkward for either writer or reader.

That is, at best a writing system can be no more than a prompting device, enough to suggest to the reader what the writer had in mind, not enough to record what a writer would have said had he been speaking. As a prompter, our writing system is not bad, probably because it has grown to serve the needs of its users, and hence if anything was needed badly enough long enough something would come about. True, the accommodation would be slow; anything as rigid as a writing system, left to its own devices, can change only slowly. And perhaps now changes are in order; after all, the system was mainly developed for reading aloud or silently with lip movements; modern reading needs a rapid system, and our means of recording written thought could surely be made somewhat more elaborate without breaking down. But much deliberate overhaul of the system is probably not to be expected; fortunately, not much is needed.

NEW TOOLS, NEW TECHNIQUES

Writing has led, also, to contributory inventions, of which the first was the dictionary. The practice started with glosses. A Roman priest working in York or Canterbury, trying to read an Old English statute, would write a Latin equivalent over a strange word; however curious he might be in the law, even a learned man could not become fluent in local jargons. And a native priest, not overly learned in Latin and Greek, would write a French or English term over a difficult Classical word. When such glossed equivalents were brought together into a list, the result was a simple two-language dictionary—after all, the most elementary definition, after pointing, is a synonym. The first such list we know is the *Promptorum Parvulorum,* "a storehouse for children," intended for those who were trying to learn Latin, as all educated children had to. By Shakespeare's time, word books were being prepared for adults, but only for such people as merchants, women, and cottagers—gentlemen would be educated and know the words already. These books entered only hard words or rare uses. One Elisah Coles, preparing *An English Dictionary, Explaining Difficult Terms* (1685), included *horse* only as "a rope fastened to the fore-mast shrouds, to keep the sprit-sail sheats clear of the anchor-flukes," and *horse-tail* only as "an herb good for inward wounds and ulcers." In the next century the lexicographer Nathaniel Bailey included the common use of *horse*, but described the creature as "a beast well known," without indicating what it might look like or be good for. This fact, that early dictionaries were intended for fledgling users of the language, helped promote the notion that dictionaries should police usage. Presumably common folk would want to know how to talk like gentlemen, and the dictionary would help them do it, telling them how they ought to speak. And this notion has persisted; the third edition of the *New International*, an excellent book, was widely condemned because the editor described how the word *ain't* is used, and gave less attention to scolding people for using it than some reviewers felt would have been proper.

Subsequently, better philosophies of dictionaries developed, mainly on the Continent, and were imported. The basic principles are these:

> *Dictionaries should describe all aspects of all words as completely and objectively as possible.* Of course abridged dictionaries have their uses for convenience, and specialized books like medical dictionaries are imperative. Use, including usage, is part of the description of a word, but only part; mainly a dictionary should be descriptive, not prescriptive.

> *Language should be described by its use.* Language is what it is because of the way it has been used, and whatever it becomes, use will determine. The readiest way to describe language objectively is to take written citations of its past use and generalize from them. Oral use should be given equal weight and treated with like objectivity. Specialists should determine special uses; local use should be determined by local users.

All good dictionaries are now built on such principles, but not all users of dictionaries understand these practices. The *New International*, third edition, was innovative in various ways, notably that the editors tried to reflect usage by citations, as volumes like the *Oxford* have tried to reveal meaning by citation. But the public generally did not understand this; the dictionary quoted a prizefighter to show the level of usage a pugilist is likely to favor, but purists assumed that anything in the dictionary was being recommended, and they were furious that they were being told, as they supposed, to talk like "pugs." Someday, the nature of lexicography will be commonplace, but as yet dictionary theory is running ahead of the sophistication of dictionary users, so much so that most dictionary owners do not as yet know how to use their books.

Meanwhile, innovations continue. In recent decades we have had two sorts of synonym books, one that discriminates related synonyms with some care, another that suggests synonyms or alternate ways of saying something. At this writing publishers are trying to bring all three sorts of treatments, the dictionary entry, the discrimination of synonyms, and suggestions for other synonymic choices together on one page. Such books would help writers. As for usage, we have seen above that linguistic geography provides a technique for tracing the movement of language; a variation upon the technique can be used to determine usage with something like scientific accuracy

And there are new experiments. One, called *glottochronology* or *lexicostatistics* is an attempt to project backward, so that we can date linguistic events now thousands of years gone without contemporary trace. It works on an analogy with carbon dating; carbon decays at a constant and known rate, and thus the carbon remaining in a carbon-bearing object can be used to date artifacts. If the carbon is half wasted, the object is half as old as the decay rate for carbon. Similarly, some linguists believe that certain sorts of words—those for the heavenly bodies, family relationships, and the like—also decay at a steady rate. If this is true, we can determine the time lapse between stages of a language, but it may not be true, and even if it is for some sorts of words, working with a few thousand years the research worker will run out of words, especially since he must rely on statistical probabilities. Accordingly, the utility of glottochronology is uncertain, but it does suggest that dramatic new inventions continue to make language an exciting study.

Similarly, the computer has potential for language; up to now, speech has on the whole been too complex for computers, which thus far have done best with simple problems. But techniques will be improved, and as I write this, word comes that computers can now translate the simple prose used by business and science—but no poetry and no involved or thoughtful prose. The tale concerning one computer is probably apocryphal, but revealing; presented with "The spirit is willing, but the flesh is weak," it spewed out, "The whiskey is all right, but the meat is rotten." The time may yet be when FORTRAN, at present a means of giving instruction to a machine, may grow into a language —with dialects, of course—for Mother Tongue has a penchant for becoming involved in all sorts of innovations. Or the computer may have to settle for a sort of pidgin.

13

LANGUAGE
AS GROWTH

LITERATURE, RHETORIC, LEARNING, PROFESSIONS, BUSINESS

The phrase *Mother Tongue* has implications not usually attached to it. The term is as old as the fourteenth century, when Wycliffe wrote that children should be taught the law of God in *here modyr tongue*. Because *mother* is one of those words that had an uninflected genitive in Old English, and *here* is the genitive of the OE third person plural pronoun, he meant, in modern spelling, "in their mother's tongue," recognizing that a child's native speech is what he has learned from his mother—along with some of the neighboring kids. Most users of the phrase today probably mean no more by it than *native speech;* or they mean that a language can have a parent, as Proto-Indo-European can figuratively be the mother of daughter languages like English, or that culturally the native speech can be thought of as the mother of us all. But it might appropriately be used because mothers are creative, fertile, bringing forth good things that did not exist before. Language does that.

LITERATURE AND LANGUAGE

Curiously, the Mother Tongue of speakers of English, ancient as she is, continues to produce offspring. And they are highly varied. Consider literature; the "new poetry" represents a revolution in language use, although poetry is everywhere prehistoric, and in English we have written poetry since before 700 A.D. Throughout these centuries, poetry has relied on agile use of language, with a succession of conventions calculated to make language work harder and play more.

English poetry has utilized various linguistic devices; Old English notably had three. A line of poetry was bound together by alliteration; *Beowulf* contains the following:

> weox   under   wolcnum   weorðmyndum   þah

The line (it means, "he grew great under heaven, became mighty in mind") is composed of two half-lines, each with two beats, the pattern revealed by the repeated /w/ sounds. Old French used long lines knit by assonance; Middle English used rhyme and rhythm, but had also a curious symbolic system, borrowed from contemporary theology.

The notion was that God had hidden his secrets in a concatenation of puns, the Four-fold Levels of Truth, so that anything significant would be revealed through a pun, and the more exalted the idea, the more complex the pattern of puns. Consider *Rome,* in the sentence, "On the way to Rome, I knew God." On the simplest level, the geographical, the sentence would report an event during a journey to a city; Rome existed as geographical fact. On the second level, the philosophical, *Rome* symbolized the church; the statement now concerns conversion to Christianity. On the third, or theological level, *Rome* implied Christ, so that the statement now delineates another sort of experience, probably mystical and soul-renewing. At the highest level, the anagogical, almost anything could happen, but *Rome* might mean eternal truth or ineffable joy. Further one should ask, What happens to the other words in the sentence? What does *way* mean? Dante tells us his great reform took place after he got out of "the right way" in a "dark wood" inhabited by symbolic beasts—clearly *way* here has at least two meanings. In what sense is *knew* used, and what is *God?* The reader of a medieval poem must ask such questions, although because this is a paragraph not a book, I shall not attempt to answer them.

Such shifts in language as a creative power in poetry continued. Marlowe's "mighty line" relied on language use; of Helen he asks: "Was this the face that launched a thousand ships/ and burnt the topless towers of Ilium?" And tough, subtle, and multiple use of language lives in Shakespeare. Macbeth, newly a murderer, says his hand will "The multitudinous seas incarnadine/ Making the green one red." Will the hand make "the green, one red," or will it make the green one, red?" Doubtless Shakespeare was aware of both and meant both. In the seventeenth century with people like John Donne and George Herbert, a sort of poetry flourished, relying on elaborate figures and many-leveled use of language, which Samuel Johnson termed "metaphysical." Donne has a lover arguing to his lass that nothing amatory they may do can affront nature because their bloods have already been inextricably blended by the flea that has bitten both of them. Metaphysical poetry was followed in the eighteenth century with verse using what was called "poetic diction"; by it birds became "wanderers of heaven," "the plumy race," "the tenants of the sky" and even the barnyard fowls were "the household of feathery people," the "female train" of the "crested cock." Such fancies were in turn replaced by a "natural" school promoted by Wordsworth, who recommended that poetry be written in "a selection of language really used by men." Poets of the nineteenth century entertained a concern for the sensuous use of words, as in Keats' "the blushful Hippocrene,/ With beaded bubbles winking at the brim,/ And purple-stained mouth." Later arose the imagist school in France and elsewhere—but this book should not be a history of poetry, and a history of what writers have tried to do with language approaches that.

For the current movement, one might notice the title of a recent volume of verse by James Masson Gunn, *God Wrests*. The phrase induces a flood of associations. God labored six days creating the universe, and *rested* from his labors. The State *rests*—the Establishment has done its best to convict us; or the defense *rests,* nothing more can be done for us. Is God laid to *rest?* GOD: REQUIESCAT IN PACE. Is God offering comfort—"God *rest* ye merry, gentlemen." A couched spear is in ar*rest;* a person deprived of liberty is ar*rested;* so is a disease no longer threatening. But the word here is spelled *wrest.* How does God wrench things from their natural orders? What is the nature of God, that his actions *wrest,* or do they not, normally? The word *wrestler* comes from *wrest;* is God then still *wrest*ling, and with that ancient evil from "chaos and old night?"

In short, many modern poets try to use language to communicate directly—Gunn, who was a composer before he turned to verse, writes me that he handles words as he would the units of music. Such poets hope by association to move minds without the intervention of syntax, employing words to suggest, not logically but intuitively. Their method is rather like those of the poets who toyed with the Four-fold Levels of Truth; as Dante was relying on the many-leveled nature of God, they rely on many-leveled language, and both sorts of poets seek a super-rational truth. Their leader, of course, has been T. S. Eliot, whose *The Waste Land* had worldwide impact. He suggests that the aridity of modern society reflects the wasteland of Arthurian romance, induced by the emasculation of its leaders, but to do this he pillages the lore of the Classics, Western and Oriental, embodying his insights in the many-leveled use of words. Such poetry is rather like the medieval search for truth, except that after the modern manner it is unordered rather than systematic. It replaces the symbolics of theology with the symbolic power of language.

Something similar has happened throughout literature. Some plays seem to have been concocted to exploit the shock value of selected Old English words, but ignoring them, one can still observe that literary experiment has been instinct with language. Hemingway used a low-keyed, hard-mannered language, both in word choice and sentence structure, as part of a new honesty that redirected a generation of fiction writers. Faulkner's rich and subtle use of language accounted for at least as much of his impact as did the amoral Snopes and the ingenious rapes that drew comment. The theater of the absurd, black humor, the Kafkaesque satires, the bitter blend of comic realism and phantasy in John Hawkes's *The Beetle Leg* and in John Barth's *Giles Goatboy,* the disillusioned wit of the Salingers and Donleavys, the involuted subtley of Vladimir Nabokov as in *Pale Fire* and *Ada*—almost every genre of modern writing has undergone revolutions, and without exception an alerted sense of language has provided some of the new tools. Less spectacularly, but quite as surely, a growing sense of language has invigorated nonfiction, as any study of the writings of Rebecca West, Rachel Carson, and dozens of others will reveal.

Rhetoric has recently revived, with new turns toward language, including attention to what is often called *specificity,* the degree to which a term is and should be concrete or specific. Modern prose is more sharply pinned down with precise and vigorous terminology than was the writing of earlier centuries, and partly because modern students of writing have examined the values of both the general and the specific in writing. Likewise, large aspects of writing have drawn attention. The paragraph has been achieved. Older prose writers like Milton and Dryden are now difficult reading, in part because they were nearly innocent of paragraphing in the modern sense. Great nineteenth-century prose writers—Macaulay, Froude, Newman, Ruskin, Arnold, Stevenson, and many others—knew about paragraphs and practiced them, but paragraph structure has become surer and paragraph practice clearer and more pointed in our time. Most good nonfiction writers produce good paragraphs with great consistency, although the competence has not yet gone much beyond professional writers. I have heard many a parent rebuke his child, "Johnny, don't say *ain't*," but I have yet to hear a parent say, "But Johnny, you are not talking in paragraphs." One reason may be that Johnny has not yet heard about paragraphs in any real way, and another may be that his parent has not. But they both will; good rhetoric is growing in this country, and growing partly through language.

LANGUAGE, BOTH INFLATED AND DEFLATED

But not all of Mother Tongue's births have been felicitous. What used to be called "black sheep" are traditional in the best of families, and not all linguistic offspring have been either artistic or witty. In fact, many observers warn that modern English is being engulfed in a sort of linguistic sludge that debilitates the nation. As one news magazine editor put it, "The English language ain't well. Abused and confused by Americans, it is turning into no-English, a flabby hodge-podge of slang and jargon that don't mean much to nobody. . . . Linguistic chaos exists everywhere . . . throughout the great oral wastes of the nation." As I write, this jeremiad is more than ten years old, but the magazine that published it is still using the flabby hodge-podge to edit with, and doing very well.

One has the feeling that we must here be in the presence of over-inflated prose, but the writer was talking about something real. Representative James A. Quigley was justly disturbed about what he called "creeping federalese" when he read the following into the *Congressional Record*:

The Board of Commissioners took the position that as the Secretary of the Army necessarily would consider the board's recommendation against the legislation and the board's reasons for its action, in connection with

both references, the advising you of the board's views and recommenda-
tions should be delayed until final action by the Secretary of the Army
on your reference to the Department of Defense.

Meanwhile, a corporate executive was explaining why his company had
lost money—although he used no such direct terms. What he said was
"the slowdown in order activity," involving a "dollar factor increase"
had impeded "the inertia of reactivating . . . implementative pro-
grams" (which, incidentally, had never been activated anyhow). For the
"current annum," he assured, "we expect to steadily increase our pene-
tration into this market," especially since "with relatively limited ex-
posure to date, our superior performance capabilities and adaptability
to a wide range of portable, mobile, and airborne environments have
generated rapid and far-reaching customer acceptance." What he meant
was that the company had lost money because people would not buy
its products but now the management hoped to sell more. Meanwhile,
in the Middle West a legislator was warning that "the banker's pockets
are bulging with the sweat of honest workingmen," and "Milwaukee
is the golden egg that the rest of the state wants to milk." A sheriff,
squabbling with the county commissioners charged that they "could
not see their nose despite their face."

Doubtless this sort of thing blossoms the more readily in our nouveau-
riche, recently learned society, but if anyone supposes it is restricted
to American English he should read Sir Ernest Gowers' *Plain Words:
Their ABC* (1954; published in England as *The Complete Plain
Words*). Gowers quotes the following from a British scientist:

> Reservers that are occupied in continuous uni-directional adjustment of
> a disorder are no longer available for use in the ever-varying interplay
> of organism and environment in the spontaneity of mutual synthesis.

The bureaucrats do no better, observing, "Unfortunately a complete
breakdown of British trade is not possible," and "Statistics have been
issued of the population of the United States, broken down by age and
sex." For this sort of officialese he has coined the happy term, *pudder*,
and he notes, without using the phrase, that pudder promulgates
pudder. It seems a department sent the following instructions:

> Every woman by whom . . . a claim for maternity benefits is made shall
> furnish evidence that she has been, or that it is expected that she will be,
> confined by means of a certificate in accordance with the rules. . . .

One woman dutifully replied, "In accordance with your instructions I have given birth to twins in the enclosed envelope."

One of Gowers' best collections concerns the jargonic use of *bottleneck*. The word's finest hour may have come in England during World War II, when many commodities were in short supply. One writer warned that there were "bottlenecks ahead," including "the biggest bottleneck"—although of course if a literal bottleneck is big enough there will be no figurative bottleneck. Some observers cautioned that "bottlenecks must be ironed out," and that there was danger of an "overriding bottleneck," a "most drastic bottleneck," along with a bottleneck that was "particularly far-reaching and decisive." There was even a "bottleneck in bottlenecks," so that the whole lead to a "world-wide bottleneck," even to a "vicious circle of interdependent bottlenecks."

The news-magazine editor quoted above, in his zeal to save Mother Tongue from a fate worse than death, had apparently let his filial devotion color his reportorial objectivity, but he had nonetheless observed something. If a reader will compare modern bureaucratic prose with the superb letters penned by Horace Walpole and John Keats, he must be struck with the mediocrity of some current writing. If one compares the superb eloquence of an Edmund Burke with the Wisconsin legislator who charged that "This guy was down in Illinois under a consumed name," he would draw similar inferences.

But these are the wrong comparisons. Formerly, but few people were educated enough to write; they were mainly selected people, many of them selected for their intelligence, and if they were educated at all they were mostly educated well. They were the only people whose writings we can now read. Our philosophy of education is different; we have tried to educate everybody, and accordingly half-learned persons—who can read and write but cannot use the language very well—find themselves in imposing positions, or at least in official posts where they make official pronouncements, albeit in execrable English. This way of life may be bad. One assumes the journalist—the one who fears that American English has become a "flabby hodgepodge"—would believe so; many of us would dissent, in the hope that trying to educate all the people has advantages that outweigh its other effects—such as the growth of pudder—that everything has the faults of its virtues, and that universal education inevitably leads to some debasing of official prose. The fact is that the legislator who wanted to consider "egress and degress from the building" would not have been delivering a Burkean address or penning a Declaration of Independence. His counterpart two centuries ago would not have known how to read and write.

Undoubtedly the average modern educator, the average modern scientist, writes poorer prose than did either Charles Darwin or Thomas Henry Huxley. That is, there is more bad writing published today than was printed a century ago; most potential composers of flabby prose were not educated in that day, and if they were, what they published —if anything—is no longer read. On the other hand, good modern prose is palpably as good as the best prose of a century ago, and there is much more of it. Modern writing has excellences not always noticed, and the growth of prose in the twentieth century stems in part from the creativity of modern speech.

14

LANGUAGE
AS GOD

"In the beginning God created the heaven and earth. . . . So God created man in His own image, male and female created He them." But we have seen that man could not become what we call human until he had language of a sort, and that man has been making language ever since, growing it as he uses it. Whatever "created" implies in the Biblical account, this sort of creation goes on, and language must be one of the media. Is it also one of the creators?

We have seen that at least in a limited way it is. Scientists develop words for diseases and refine the use of these words; doctors can work better and even think better because they have such words. Mechanics can repair a car better because they have exact terms for automotive parts. But does language direct the working of the mind also in larger ways?

Many thinkers believe it does, that inevitably it must. One of them was Benjamin Lee Whorf, an engineer who became interested in language. Studying the Hopi, he concluded that although these Southwest Indians had very sophisticated philosophic notions they did not have the concept of time common in Western culture, of something continuously flowing through the past into the present and toward the future. Instead he observed what he calls *manifesting*. The universe is conceived as potentials, of which some become manifest. The attention is on reality, on the certainty or uncertainty of reality, although all reality is presumably inevitable eventually and is always possible. One does not say in Hopi, "It is hot in the summer," but "Heat exists summering." That which is always potential becomes manifest within certain circumstances. As Whorf put it, "time disappears and space is altered, so that it is no longer the homogeneous and instantaneous timeless space of our supposed intuition or of Classical Newtonian mechanics." In other words, our fundamental notions do not necessarily represent realities; they are the creation of our minds working through language. "Newtonian space, time, and matter are no intuitions," he writes. They come from "culture and language," and "that is where Newton got them." Being a scientist he saw all this for its impact on scientific thinking and on science itself; he had to conclude that science is not objective truth. It is the logical development that has grown out of Western ideas as embodied in Western culture and controlled through Western use of language. A science built upon Hopi concepts would be a different science, and Whorf entertained the possibility that it might have been a better one.

WHO OR WHAT IS CREATING WHOM?

If Whorf is right, then man is creating himself in his own image, the image mirrored in his language. We should notice that Whorf's thesis —often called the Whorf-Sapir thesis, because Whorf got many of his ideas from his professor, Edward Sapir—has not won entire acceptance. Whorf had little formal anthropological or linguistic training; scholars have detected him in some errors, and many linguists believe he has pushed his thesis too far. But within limits he cannot be wrong.

Consider the evidence of color. Color has an objective reality; it is determined by wave length, and presumably these waves are the same everywhere. But people do not see colors in the same way, and the ways they see tints and shades change with the color-terms they use. One body of speakers may see four or five colors, such as red, orange, yellow, green, and blue, while others see two or three with tints and shades and still others see a dozen colors. The spectrum is a continuum, but various peoples divide it differently, and consequently give names to larger or smaller parts, to overlapping parts or parts within parts, and they then see and think in accordance with the names. Russian has no word for blue, but two words are often translated light blue and dark blue. French has no word to cover what we mean by *brown,* but uses three words, *marron* and *brun* and sometimes *jaune.* The Hindi word *pila* is often translated *yellow* or *orange,* but also as *brown, tan, cinnamon,* and the like. And these are all IE languages; in other languages the spread is even greater.

Recently we have become aware that our ideas and our actions may be more directed by our emotions than we had supposed, and that words change feelings. Many a Black child has reported that his first rude shock came when somebody called him a "dirty nigger." Negroes are not necessarily any dirtier than so-called white people, but indisputably many objects get whiter when they are clean and darker when they are dirty. By combining *dirty* with *nigger,* a word that was originally only a color designation (Latin *niger* meaning *black*), this becomes an insult that harms people who use it and those on whom it is used. An elderly gentleman with a weak heart and a strong hatred of all social reform detested Franklin Roosevelt so much that his doctor ordered him never to be in a society where the name of the then president might be uttered, lest the sound prove fatal to him. All advertisers know so well that favorable or unfavorable sentiments can be aroused by certain words that they fill their notices with pretty people and pretty phrases.

Nor is the control that language exercises over us restricted to our known mental processes. Psychiatrists have become so aware of the working of language in the subconscious mind that they have cultivated techniques to promote curative language in their patients and to thwart noxious terms. They have found that the deeper reaches of the mind will use puns and figures of speech to obscure old emotional scars.

Even grammar must have its impact on its users. IE grammar made strong use of time in the verb, and this awareness may have helped the IE peoples to organize reality by time, and even to become great achievers. Some languages have verbs oriented toward truth in evidence; the speaker of such a language, whenever he selects a verb form, must decide on what authority he speaks. He must indicate that he himself experienced what he reports—he saw it, heard it, felt it. Or he can indicate that he is relaying information for what it may be worth, that he does not know how trustworthy the reporter might be. Obviously, schooling oneself to make such decisions from infancy could not fail to affect the way in which speakers of the language use their minds.

Similarly, in some speech place dominates. A speaker using a noun must indicate whether or not an object can be reached by one of his senses—he has it in his possession, or can see it, hear it, or smell it. Otherwise, he may indicate that he cannot sense the object, but he believes he knows where it is, and it is not far. An object not so identifiable is thus far off or uncertainly known. Such decisions were not forced upon the speaker of an IE language, but he was often required to decide the sex of an object. One cannot help speculating what might have been the course of Western history and modern thinking if IE languages had been geared to a system that required decisions about space rather than decisions about sex.

THE MEDIUM AND THE MESSAGE

Even the medium of language has impact. When language was only oral, ideas could spread directly only within the limits of the human voice and the proximity of the listener. Even the arts were influenced by the limitations of auditors. Early poetry was formulaic, because through patterns it could be remembered, and through patterns it could readily be devised. We are told that when Beowulf, in the epic by that name, killed a monster and freed the people from scourge, the court poet celebrated the event on the spot with a poem. The effusion is not preserved, but we know how he could do this. As has been mentioned, Old English poetry employed two half-lines knit together by alliteration and adorned with tropes, many of them conventional. Suppose the poet started, in a modern equivalent, with "Beowulf the Hero!" He now has his first half-line, and he needs another, to be made up of two main stresses, at least one of them alliterating with B or H. A number of conventional epithets would serve; while he was devising the next line of his impromptu composition, he might complete the first line by saying, "hard under the helm," a compliment to a grim fighter, or "breaker of rings."

Thus the fact that language was oral colored its artistic use and the participation of people in art. When writing came in, a new body of literary conventions grew because distribution no longer depended upon people listening, but upon people who could read, upon the availability of writing materials, upon the fact that the word did not vanish once it was spoken. Printing brought other impacts of language upon man. In the days of oral transmission, nothing could survive unless the subject was so popular that in every generation somebody would love it or treasure it enough to commit it to memory. With writing, once something was recorded it could survive regardless of limited popularity. On the other hand, much could not be written or reproduced; to be worthy of copying, an original had to be worth the parchment and the labors of the scriptorium. With printing the audience became so vast that highly specialized matters could be dealt with —there would always be some readers somewhere. And now radio, television, and computers bring new conventions of composition, and with them different impacts upon human beings. Language has subtle and pervasive ways to alter men, most of them unnoticed by the victims, or the beneficiaries.

Thus language may be more godlike than we know. Language has always been the servant of deities; praise and prayers alike were uttered in words, and written language grew as fast as it did partly because it was needed to preserve holy documents. But once it existed it turned upon its maker; from being a medium it has become in some ways the master—"when me ye fly, I am the wings." The question cannot be: Was Whorf wrong? The question has to be: Was Whorf right in many little things, or in very large ones? Language has been at least a minor lord of the mind for a long time, and in the end, whatever molds the mind shapes the future.

15

LANGUAGE
AND THE FUTURE

Prophecy is an uncertain, even a risky business. Prophets have lost their heads along with their good names, and sometimes as much for being right as for being wrong. But among fair-minded people, a prophet is as good as his prophecy, and some subjects are more open to prediction than are others. The movements of the celestial bodies are subject to precise calculation, but only if one knows enough. An individual plane crash is almost unpredictable, but generalized predictions can be made even about accidents. In the past we have known so little about language that prudent observers have attempted few predictions, and most of those who did were proven wrong by the event. Now, however, we know more and should do better.

On the whole, prophecy about language has been a gloomy affair. Formerly, even specialists did not know that change is omnipresent in language, that within limits change does no harm and is even healthy. People generally do not like change in language; it introduces something strange, or popularizes something unpopular. They deplore change, and if they detect any, they fear it is change for the worse. Fortunately, most of the time most people remain euphoriously unaware of most of the changes, but even so they are likely to conclude that language is getting worse and that the worsening will go on.

Our ancestors had little opportunity to prophesy about language because they had too little firm knowledge to reason from. They thought they knew something of the origin of language, but they were mistaken. They trusted that language had resulted from a single miracle, and that any change since that miracle was a corruption. Even when they saw that such a description did not fit the known facts, they tended not to reorient their thinking—even Webster, who had to conclude that language had grown and that any language imparted by Jehovah to Adam must have been pretty limited speech, continued to believe in the miracle as a sort of language starter, and to assume that purity should be preserved in language. He did not know how language began, nor do we, but at least we are aware of our ignorance. We are not confidently reasoning from a false assumption, that language has largely declined from a pristine perfection.

We now have sufficiently detailed records of language, covering such a long period, that we should be able to project with some confidence—in fact, we should be able to project in both directions. Early in this book I tried to extend the lines of our knowledge somewhat backward toward a beginning. Here we are concerned with the future. It all resembles the following diagram:

```
                            Projection both forward
Origin?◄─3000 B.C.◄──────── and backward based on ──────►A.D. 2000─►Future?
◄─────────────────────────── 5000 years of evidence ────────────────────►
```

That is, studying five thousand years of language we now believe we have a fundamental understanding of how language works, and can, within limits, plot its future, very much as we have projected its past to PIE and beyond. Formerly there were such chasmlike gaps in our knowledge about language that plotting a course was foolhardy. We are still bewildered by language, but from having been mostly wrong we trust we are now mostly right. Accordingly, we should do better than did our ancestors, better than did the magazine editor quoted in the previous chapter. Here are fundamental principles we should keep in mind:

Language has always changed, and presumably it always will.
Language change may result from corruption, but mainly change results in growth. At least, susceptibility to change makes language adaptable.

Language changes at varying rates; some aspects of language, like grammar, change slowly; others, like certain usages, change quite rapidly.

On the whole, language change can be plotted in curves; some will be long, slow curves; some short, sharp curves.

Drifts in language tend to be consistent; in general a change that starts quickly can stop quickly, one that is slow to build up will be slow to stop. A great movement neither starts nor stops precipitately.

Now we can get down to specifics, and first:

English in the World.   For more than a millennium, English has been a growing language. It will not stop tomorrow. Of course we do not know all of the patterns in this growth, but some are clear. English has expanded because it has been moving into new lands or sparsely settled lands; this growth will continue, probably more in Canada and Australia than in the United States, but it will go on. English has grown, also, because it has been the medium of burgeoning peoples. This sort of growth from within will continue in the United States and in some other countries. English has been growing as a second language; development will continue in India and China, and in Latin America, although how much is uncertain. That is, English, now one of the great languages of the world, has not worked through its pattern; it will continue to be a great language, and for a time will continue to expand.

Inevitably, non-linguistic events will have impacts. If China or Russia should take over politically, such dominance would alter language. As Latin Americans become more or less resentful of *Yanquis,* linguistic drifts will vary. What the Arabs do with their oil, and what the Japanese do with it, or without it, will have their echoes in speech. But such changes are slow, and less permeating than most people suppose; to a remarkable degree language goes its own way. Even conquest has but limited effect; American English is growing in Japan because of American music, American mass media, and American cultural patterns, not much because of American occupation.

Grammar.   Grammar will change slowly. For thousands of years English has been moving from synthesis toward analysis in grammar. This trend will not be reversed in the near future. One prominent evidence of this drift, the loss of inflection, is mostly complete; the making of prepositions seems to have declined. On the other hand, we are still making phrasal verbs, apparently in a rather lively fashion; analytic growth of that sort will continue, although perhaps at a reduced rate. Grammar changes so slowly, is so complex, and in many ways is so little understood that to make a composite estimate is to dabble in uncertainties, but we might plausibly guess that the movement from synthesis toward analysis in English grammar is now on the decline, but will continue in many of its trends for a long time.

Vocabulary. Vocabulary will expand in size and will diversify, becoming more specific and technical in many areas; it will experience some dramatic growth but will show no great change in the great body of terms. English vocabulary has been multiplying ever since we have records of it, and for more than five hundred years quite rapidly. It will not stop tomorrow. In general, patterns already described, especially in Chapter 8, will continue. We shall go on making terms from Latin and Greek syllables, but compounding will continue to decline. Areas of growing interest will balloon, resulting in what I have called nova in the language; for example, the fields of social planning, underwater exploration, and mental health will contribute to the vocabulary. Space terms have flowered, and they will flourish more if families start moving into space as the vocabulary grew when in the nineteenth century British colonials moved into India. Acronyms will continue at least for the present, but that fad flared up only recently; we do not yet know whether acronyms will provide a short curve that is now near its zenith or whether the curve will flatten out and continue for a long time. Meanwhile, most English words have been in the language since before PIE, or were borrowed rather early; few of them will disappear but many of them will alter old uses or develop new ones, and some of these individual uses can appear almost overnight. We will continue to borrow words from any language whose people enter extensively into our lives. Chinese, Japanese, Russian, Hindi, and Arabic will provide more loan words, but sporadically, and the totals will be small.

Pronunciation. Individual changes in pronunciation will be few, but spreads of pronunciation will change extensively. Sounds change slowly; the Great English Vowel Shift took centuries, the changes reflected in Grimm's Law still more centuries. Not many new sounds will appear in English, and few will die out. Most individual words in the various dialects will alter little. On the other hand, the whole pattern of English pronunciation has shifted greatly in the last thousand years because of the geographical and social shifts of its speakers. Such changes will continue to expand at the expense of British English. Within a generation or so, more persons will speak the relatively few Australian dialects than the very numerous British dialects. In the United States, urban dialects will increase at the expense of rural dialects, West Coast and Southern speech at the expense of New England and the upper Middle West dialects.

Socially accepted dialects will increase at the expense of less fashionable speech, and this change raises interesting questions. In the past, language has tended to break up, to form new dialects and to elaborate old ones. But now the forces of standardization, operating through the schools, the mass media, and the fluidity of a shifting population, are pulling the language together. Have we passed a watershed in language, so that advanced civilization unifies language whereas earlier civilization fractured it? As yet one cannot say, but meanwhile there are more limited uncertainties. Consider Black English. With every generation more black children learn Standard English; more black families mingle in white communities. This shift should reduce the prevalence of Black English. On the other hand, as Blacks acquire more help from modern medicine—which for various reasons has often been denied them—their longevity will increase and their percentage of the population will grow. Will these trends roughly cancel each other, or will Black English pronunciations increase or decline? At the moment one hesitates to predict, but on the whole one can observe that broadly speaking, English pronunciations will change only slowly, but that some changes will be rapid and considerable. They will be local, depending upon the geographical and social shifts of the population.

Usage.   Broadly, usage is highly predictable; specifically, it is not predictable at all. On the whole, the more usage changes the more it is the same thing. Old cruxes will be forgotten, but new ones will arise, to be challenged acrimoniously but not for long. There will always be language change, and this change will affect individual locutions; individual persons will feel that these changes are bad, that they are ruining our precious heritage of language, that the Mother Tongue is

becoming a hodgepodge of nonsense. Then the whole internecine warfare will be forgotten and a new set of usages condemned as barbarous
will replace the old ones, and the new generation of purists will con-
demn the new instances of slang and "bad grammar" with a righteous-
ness reminiscent of their forebears. That seems to be the way of mankind; the whole brouhaha never involves more than a fraction of one
percent of the language anyhow.

Not much can be predicted about usage problems; new occasions for
looking down purist noses, and even for taboos, can crop up almost
anywhere. A few trends can be observed. Lately words involving sex
and scatology have been gaining respectability, and this trend will probably continue for a while, although there must be limits; not many
terms are involved, and when they are all accepted for anything, how
can the movement go any further? And some day there will be a coun-
termovement. We can expect to have more shifting of terms for ethnic
groups; minorities are readily the butts of cheap humor and even of
insult, and they are likely to be supersensitive. We can expect more
new terms and more castigation of old ones. As for individual locutions, the battles over *ain't* and *he don't* are likely to go on. There is
likely to be uncertainty about terms for women, *Mrs.* and *Miss* as
against *Ms.* (pronounced /miz/), or something else. On the other hand
the teapot-tempest over *like* and *as* seems to have blown over, as has
the concern for *may* and *can,* for *shall* and *will.* The next crux is anybody's guess; most of the young people who read this sentence will
never have known that there was once in this country great division
as to whether *rations* was pronounced /rejšnz/ or /ræšənz/, whether
khaki was to be pronounced /kæki/ or /kɑki/. We know that fights
over usage we shall always have with us, but that they will be transient
and largely unpredictable.

Literature, Jargon, and *Officialese.*   In all these, language will function very much as it has, although the details will differ. Language has
always provided instruments for new artistic movements, and it will
continue to do so, perhaps now more than ever because language is
so much the subject of research—and in spite of their superficial con-
flicts, art and learning, education and scholarship are closely interknit.
They even have overlapping adherents. And as bureaucrats, professional practitioners, modestly educated technicians, and semi-learned
businessmen grow in number, we can scarcely expect jargon and offi-

cialese to decline. Of course there will be shifts; the jargon of space-men can be expected to diverge from the cant of beauticians, but the principles are likely to continue. Only the terms will change.

Meanwhile, we can trust Mother Tongue. She has never been unfaithful, or wanting when she was needed, although she has occasionally presumed upon supposedly female privileges to be a bit perverse and inexplicable. But on the whole she has been a good helpmeet to man, and like others of her sex, her power should never be underestimated.

Appendix

COMMON VOWELS AND DIPHTHONGS*

/a/	as in	*ask* /ask/ in many dialects
/ɑ/	as in	*hot* /hɑt/
/æ/	as in	*hat* /hæt/
/ɑi/	as in	*ride* /rɑid/
/ɑʊ/	as in	*house* /hɑʊs/, some dialects
/æʊ/	as in	*house* /hæʊs/, some dialects
/e/	as in	*get* /get/
/ej/	as in	*gate* /gejt/
/ə/	as in	*about* /əbɑʊt/, *under* /əndər/
/ər/	as in	*girl* /gərl/, some dialects
/ɝ/	as in	*girl* /gɝl/, some dialects
/i/	as in	*pit* /pit/
/ɨ/	as in	*gill* /gɨl/, some dialects
/ij/	as in	*heat* /hijt/
/iʊ/	as in	*few* /fiʊ/
/o/	as in	*open* /opən/
/oi/	as in	*boil* /boil/

*For descriptions and variations, see pp. 15–19.

177

/ou/ as in *boat* /bout/
/ɔ/ as in *hawk* /hɔk/
/u/ as in *boot* /but/
/ʊ/ as in *put* /pʊt/
/ʌ/ as in *putt* /pʌt/, more stressed than /ə/

COMMON AMERICAN CONSONANTS*

/b/ as in *bib* /bib/
/č/ as in *church* /čʌrč/
/d/ as in *did* /did/
/f/ as in *if* /if/
/g/ as in *go* /gou/
/h/ as in *he* /hij/
/j/ as in *you* /ju/
/k/ as in *kick* /kik/
/l/ as in *lily* /lili/
/m/ as in *my* /mɑi/
/n/ as in *no* /nou/
/ŋ/ as in *king* /kiŋ/
/p/ as in *pot* /pɑt/
/r/ as in *roar* /rour/
/s/ as in *sip* /sip/
/š/ as in *ship* /šip/
/t/ as in *tight* /tɑit/
/v/ as in *van* /væn/
/w/ as in *way* /wej/
/z/ as in *zeal* /zijl/
/ž/ as in *measure* /mežər/
/θ/ as in *thin* /θin/
/ð/ as in *these* /ðijz/
/χ/ (voiceless palatal fricative, lost)
/ɣ/ (voiced palatal fricative, lost)

* For descriptions, see pp. 19–22.

Index